C000050605

GRESLEY'S
B17s

PETER TUFFREY

GREAT NORTHERN

ACKNOWLEDGEMENTS

I am grateful for the assistance received from the following people: Roger Arnold, Ben Brooksbank, Doug Brown, David Burrill, John Chalcraft, Paul Chancellor, Peter Crangle, David Dippie, David Joy, John Law, Hugh Parkin, Bill Reed, Andrew, Rachel and Sue Warnes.

Gratitude should also be expressed to my son Tristram Tuffrey for his general help and encouragement throughout the project.

Unless otherwise stated, all photographs from author's collection.

Great Northern Books Limited
PO Box 1380, Bradford, BD5 5FB
www.greatnorthernbooks.co.uk

© Peter Tuffrey 2021

Every effort has been made to acknowledge correctly and contact the copyright holders of material in this book. Great Northern Books Ltd apologises for any unintentional errors or omissions, which should be notified to the publisher.

All rights reserved. No part of this book may be reproduced in any form or by any means without permission in writing from the publisher, except by a reviewer who may quote brief passages in a review.

ISBN: 978-1-912101-26-9

Design and layout: David Burrill

CIP Data
A catalogue for this book is available from the British Library

INTRODUCTION

In the ranks of locomotive classes produced by Sir Nigel Gresley, the B17 4-6-0 could be described as being mid-table, or bottom half, to borrow a football analogy which seems appropriate, given many class members' association with the sport. The design process was difficult and drawn out, whilst the appearance was handsome, if flawed thanks to the small tender. For around 20 years, the B17s performed well on most of the top expresses in East Anglia and on the Cambridge line from Liverpool Street, with only accusations of rough riding against them. After the introduction of British Railway Standard Class 'Britannia' Pacifics in the early 1950s, the class was left to drift until amongst the early steam withdrawals as BR's Modernisation Plan came into effect during the late 1950s.

This CV does not compare favourably to such classes as the A4 and A3 Pacifics, or V2 Class 2-6-2s, yet this was never the intention of Gresley. The B17s were built to meet a pressing need under extreme restrictions and arguably filled the void more than adequately until relieved by a robust and thought-out class, which would have occurred under Gresley if the Depression and Second World War had not intervened. Therefore, the B17 Class is worthy of study for the role the engines played in the history of rail traction in East Anglia (not forgetting the large group on the ex-Great Central Main Line for a time) and their position in Gresley's body of work.

The design of the B17 Class was largely formed thanks to events in the mid-19th century. When many of the lines were constructed in East Anglia, little thought was given to any future requirements of train weights and locomotive size. Therefore, many bridges could not withstand much stress on the structures. Furthermore, revenue was generally low and this handicapped any improvements that might have been made to the infrastructure.

By the end of the First World War, the railways were in a run-down state and matters had improved little up to the Grouping. The ex-Great Eastern Railway lines were taken over by the London & North Eastern Railway which was the second largest of the 'big four', though not in profitability terms. Some 1,336 GER locomotives were absorbed by the LNER and the principal express passenger type was the S.D. Holden S69 (LNER B12) Class 4-6-0, with support provided by the 'Claud Hamilton' (S46, D56, H88 – LNER D14, D15, D16) Class 4-4-0s.

On the Great Eastern Section of the LNER, train weights were raising in line with others across the country, with particular strain placed on locomotives by the continental boat trains that ran from Liverpool Street station to Harwich, Parkeston, etc. The B12s were struggling under these loads and the running department requested a more powerful engine.

King's Cross drawing office was delegated the task of producing a design incorporating three cylinders driving the middle axle, a boiler working at 200 lb per sq. in. and an axle load of 17 tons. Several plans were submitted to Gresley, yet all failed to meet his approval and Doncaster Works was asked to take over. The drawing office there also reached a dead end and the North British Locomotive Company was set on the job. They too could not meet the specification, though the design was accepted and ten ordered were built at the Glasgow works in 1928. These initial B17s proved troublesome in service as frame cracks kept appearing and several modifications were required before the situation was remedied to a manageable point.

Despite these problems, the design was thought capable enough to be perpetuated and Darlington soon had an order for 27 in hand, with the NBLC penalised for not meeting the target specifications, as well as delivering late. All of the new engines were fitted with Great Eastern-type tenders, although some were dispatched to work on the former Great Central main line, taking over from older 4-6-0s and 4-4-0s. Two small orders were placed at Darlington in early 1932 and late 1933 before a final batch of 14 appeared from the works in 1936 and Robert Stephenson & Co. completed the class with 11 engines in 1937. The first 48 locomotives were named after country houses in the LNER's territory, whilst the remaining 23 took those of football teams in the areas served by the company. Several changes occurred subsequently, including the adoption of regimental names from the army.

The B17s reached the end of the 1930s at work in the GE Section and GC Section, with the locomotives mainly at work on express passenger trains, but also some freight duties. As a publicity venture, two class members had been fitted with streamlined casing in the style of the A4 Class Pacifics to inaugurate the new 'East Anglian' express in 1937.

During the war years, the B17s suffered as much as the other LNER classes with lack of adequate maintenance and scarcity of materials. Class members could spend several months out of traffic awaiting attention at Stratford Works. In an effort to keep engines serviceable, the working boiler pressure was reduced from 200 to 180 lb per sq. in. This was not conducive to providing the steam needed to work 500-ton trains then prevailing all over the system. As a result, the B17s were moved in and out of the ex-GC Section in favour of more powerful Pacifics and V2s.

Following Gresley's death in 1941, Edward Thompson became Chief Mechanical Engineer of the LNER and began to implement his own plans for the company's locomotive stock. Specifically, this meant complete standardisation, with parts and types for several tasks, to replace large numbers of locomotives. With the B17s being younger than most, the class was scheduled for retention, but in a rebuilt form. Two cylinders were to be used with a diagram 100A boiler, then fitted to the new B1 Class – in fact a development of the B17 diagram 100 – amongst other sundry alterations. Twenty rebuilds were initially authorised and the first occurred in 1945, yet only ten were completed up to Nationalisation when the project was cancelled. The changed engines were reclassified B2.

As spare boilers for the B17s had been used and replacements were becoming necessary during the war, the decision was made to fit diagram 100A boilers while retaining the original features of the class. Just before Nationalisation, trials were conducted between a B17 so fitted and a B2, with the tests finding the B17 to be the superior engine. This likely contributed to the discontinuation of the B2 rebuilds.

Even though many B17s were saved from becoming two-cylinder locomotives, the superiority of the two-cylinder BR Standard Class 7 'Britannia' Pacifics displaced Gresley's engines off the main expresses between Liverpool Street, Ipswich and Norwich. The class managed to retain the Cambridge traffic, both on the ex-GE and ex-GNR routes, with increasing numbers of class members gathering at the depot. B17s also continued to work the cross-country boat trains – which called at Liverpool, Manchester, Sheffield, Lincoln and Parkeston Quay – for a time, although the class became extinct on the ex-GCR main line in the early 1950s. In their final days, most of the class members were focussed on secondary expresses, local trains and freight services. The first B17 was withdrawn in 1952, though not until 1958 was a larger number sent to the scrapyard. No. 61668 *Bradford City* was the last engine in service when finally condemned in late summer 1960.

*Gresley's B17*s captures the life of the class from introduction in 1928 through to withdrawal, using over 180 superb colour and black and white images. Almost all the class members are illustrated in both LNER and BR periods, with a small section devoted to the briefly used Thompson numbering scheme. The ten B2s are also featured as part of the collection.

The images show the locomotives at work from the lineside, as well as at stations, sheds and workshops. Some of the places included are: Liverpool Street station; Stratford; Romford; Parkeston; Ipswich; Norwich; Yarmouth; Neasden; Leicester; Nottingham; Sheffield; Doncaster.

Although perhaps largely unknown to the general public, thanks to A3 no. 4472 *Flying Scotsman* and A4 no. 4468 *Mallard*, etc, some enthusiasts remember the B17s fondly and two projects are currently underway to build a pair of new engines. Hopefully, this collection aids their noble cause by generating a more widespread interest in this class and elevates the B17s into the top half of the league table ranking Gresley's locomotives.

Peter Tuffrey
Doncaster, June 2020

Above NO. 2800 – NORTH BRITISH LOCOMOTIVE COMPANY WORKS, GLASGOW
No. 2800 *Sandringham* as new from the NBLC's workshops in early December 1928.

Below NO. 2800 – TRUMPINGTON
A short distance south of Cambridge at Trumpington, no. 2800 *Sandringham* has a modest train bound for the aforementioned city on 31st July 1934.

Above **NO. 2800 – STRATFORD**

Although numbered first in the B17 class sequence, as well as the NBLC works list, no. 2800 *Sandringham* was in fact the third member of the class to be completed by the company. The engine was handed over to the LNER at Eastfield shed, Glasgow, on the 7th December 1928. Yet, for a period of around a month, no. 2800 remained there until thoroughly run in, allowing any defects to be caught before allocated to Stratford. The locomotive is pictured there, likely at the works, during an open day during the early 1930s. Such events were particularly common across the LNER, as funds were raised for various railwaymen's and local charities. As the first B17, no. 2800 *Sandringham* would have been 'in demand' for an appearance at such events and was noted as being present at a similar open day at Hunslet, Leeds, in 1935. No. 2800 is next to a, perhaps new, third class sleeping carriage, dating the picture around 1931/1932 following the type's introduction to services on the LNER. Also, the engine's number is now applied to the cabside and was moved around late 1930, after the first general repair.

Opposite above **NO. 2800 – CROWLANDS**

Between Chadwell Heath and Romford on the Great Eastern main line, no. 2800 *Sandringham* has the 'Eastern Belle Pullman' at Crowlands during summer 1929. Around the turn of the century, the GER had planned to open a station serving the area around Crowlands, yet the scheme was cancelled, even though some work had been started on the platforms. At the time the area was sparsely populated, suggesting a proposed or expected housing boom did not occur; Crowlands did not see significant development until after the First World War. Crowlands signal box was relatively superfluous as the station was not built and was closed after the Second World War.

Opposite below **NO. 2801 – SPALDING STATION**

No. 2801 *Holkham* was the second B17 to be dispatched from the NBLC in early December 1928 and first allocated to Stratford shed. The first ten class members built by the NBLC wore the standard LNER passenger green livery with black and white lining, as well as black cylinders. A short-lived feature of these Scottish-built engines was the application of the number to the tender under 'LNER'. This was standard practice for most of the company's locomotives from around 1925, though this would soon be discontinued and the number was applied on the cabside. No. 2801 *Holkham* has a southbound express at Spalding station around 1929/1930.

Above NO. 2802

No. 2802 *Walsingham* was the first class member delivered to the LNER in late November 1928, though the engine was immediately returned to the NBLC. This was due to the nameplate being attached to the leading splasher, whereas LNER practice was for the driving wheel splasher to carry the plate.

Below NO. 2803

No. 2803 *Framlingham* is between duties at an unidentified location, during the mid- to late 1930s.

Above No. 2805 – PARKESTON
Parkeston shed welcomed no. 2805 *Burnham Thorpe* to the ranks early in 1929 and had the locomotive on the roster until transferred to Ipswich in May 1938. No. 2805 is in the yard of the former during the late 1930s.

Below NO. 2804
A stopping train is hauled by no. 2804 *Elveden* at an unknown location c. 1935. The motley collection of carriages includes a horse box coupled to the tender.

Opposite above NO. 2806 – WESTERFIELD STATION

A short distance north of Ipswich, Westerfield station was opened on 1st June 1859, as the Halesworth, Beccles & Haddiscoe Railway extended an earlier short section of line to Ipswich. The route was later taken over by the Great Eastern Railway, though a private company built a branch to Felixstowe in 1877, using the line east of Westerfield as a connection point. No. 2806 *Audley End* has an express at Westerfield station in the mid- to late 1930s.

Opposite below NO. 2808 – WHITTLESFORD

No. 2808 *Gunton* has a slow train to London Liverpool Street station at Whittlesford on 24th July 1933. The train had recently begun the journey from Cambridge, which was a short distance to the north.

Below NO. 2806

There was little consensus between the railway companies of Great Britain as to the brake system to use. At Grouping in 1923, the LNER inherited six companies and four used Westinghouse air brakes, whilst two had vacuum brakes. Westinghouse brakes operated through air pressure keeping the brakes off and when this reduced the brakes were activated. The competing system was vacuum brakes, where negative pressure caused the brakes to release and air pressure was needed to operate them. Both systems have advantages and disadvantages. The Great Eastern Railway was amongst the Westinghouse users and the system had been employed from at least the late 19th century. The LNER was obliged to continue to cater for both systems after Grouping and not until 1928 was the decision taken to concentrate on the vacuum method. Yet, the task of bringing all stock to conformity was to be long and arduous, resulting in the first 15 B17s being equipped with the Westinghouse pump, which is prominent here above the cylinder on no. 2806 *Audley End*.

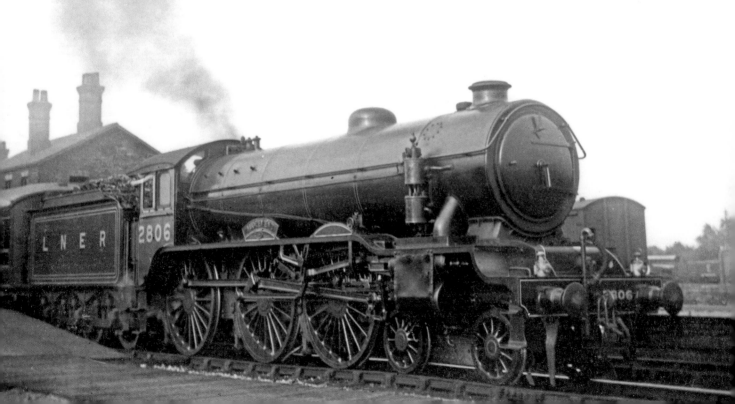

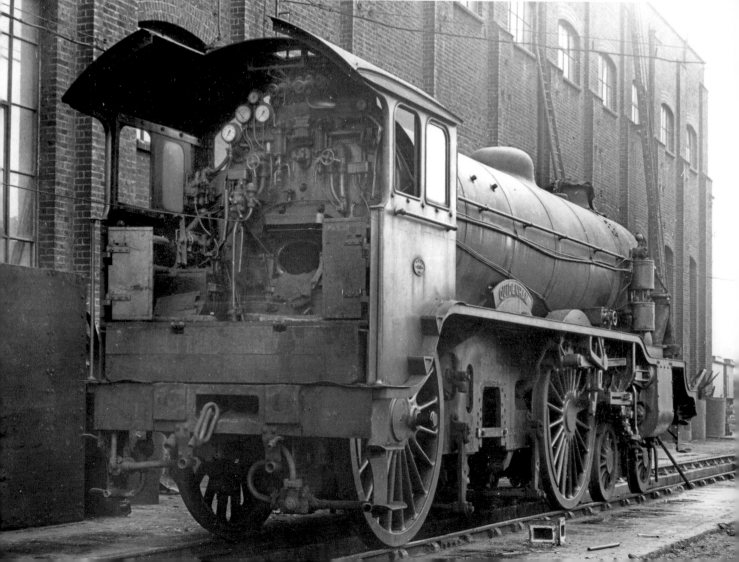

Above NO. 2808 – TOTTENHAM NORTH JUNCTION

A short distance to the south of Tottenham Hale station at Tottenham North Junction, a collision occurred on 5th October 1929 between the 05.05 express from Liverpool Street station to Norwich and the 02.45 West Green to Churchbury goods train. The latter, which was hauled by Holden J15 Class 0-6-0 no. 7938, consisted of 14 empty coal wagons and a 20-ton brake van, whilst the express was formed of 12 carriages headed by no. 2808 *Gunton*. The freight train was held at a signal and the driver thought he heard the signal move, but did not see the change, and moved off. The approaching express struck the middle group of wagons at speed and was derailed, running for a distance of 140 yards before stopping. Incredibly, the crew escaped any serious injury and the passengers also avoided any harm. No. 2808 is righted by a pair of breakdown cranes following the collision before an enthralled crowd of spectators.

Opposite above NO. 2810

The LNER experienced problems with the NBLC when ordering the first ten B17s. Namely, the company was over three months late in delivering the batch, following difficulties in completing the design satisfactorily. The LNER had graciously waved the penalties for delays in production, yet was reluctant to place a second order, despite the pleas of the NBLC. Darlington Works was given an order for 12 more locomotives in late 1928, followed by a further 15 at the end of 1929. No. 2810 *Honingham Hall* was the first of these locomotives to enter service and appeared from the shops in late August 1930. Both engine and crew have paused briefly for this photograph to be captured during the mid-1930s.

Opposite below NO. 2809 – STRATFORD WORKS

The LNER's design team struggled to create a suitable locomotive for employment in the Great Eastern Area. Stringent requirements had been set by Gresley to keep the new engines in line with the limitations of the permanent way, bridges and turntables. The proposed class had to have 25,000 lb tractive effort, three cylinders, grate area of 30 sq. ft and maximum axle load of 17 tons. When both King's Cross and Doncaster drawing offices failed, the North British Locomotive Company was employed to produce a design and one was later accepted by the LNER, although the axle load was a ton over the limit. Only ten B17s were built by the NBLC and all of these locomotives later gave trouble in service with severe fractures of the frames, due to stiff bracing. As a result, the group was fitted with new frames during the early 1930s that had strengthening around the horns and improved springs. No. 2809 *Quidenham* is at Stratford Works on 5th September 1931 in the midst of this repair, which took a particularly long time (for all the locomotives), lasting from June 1931 until mid-February 1932.

NO. 2811 – ROMFORD

No. 2811 *Raynham Hall* was celebrating a year in service during August 1931. The engine is pictured in the month, working an eastbound express near Romford.

Above and below NO. 2812 – CAMBRIDGE SHED

Located on land immediately north west of Cambridge station, the locomotive shed possessed a 55 ft turntable from at least the early 20th century. In the mid-1930s, the apparatus was upgraded to a 70 ft example, owing to frequent visits by Pacifics, during a large-scale modernisation project. This was still to come when no. 2812 *Houghton Hall* was captured on the 55 ft turntable, which was made by Ransomes & Rapier Ltd, in these two scenes, taken 22nd June 1932.

Opposite above NO. 2814 – BELSTEAD

No. 2814 *Castle Hedingham* works hard with a southbound express at Belstead, a short distance away from Ipswich, in 1931. This section of line was difficult for London-bound trains, as gradients of 1 in 120, 1 in 168 and 1 in 130 accounted for five miles south of Ipswich. The remaining five miles to Manningtree were easy, though northbound trains had a similar challenge to face. No. 2814 worked from Stratford shed for much of the first decade in service.

Opposite below NO. 2815 – AUDLEY END

An express for Liverpool Street station has burst from Audley End tunnel, which was located just north of the station, on 26th June 1931. No. 2815 *Culford Hall* is leading the train with a good head of steam. The locomotive had eight months in service at this point and was allocated from new to Stratford.

Below NO. 2813 – IPSWICH

When new from Darlington Works in October 1930, no. 2813 *Woodbastwick Hall* had the cylinder sides decorated with lined green livery and 'Class B17' underneath the number on the bufferbeam. These were both non-standard features for locomotives built and maintained on other parts of the LNER and did not reappear when the first general repair took place at Stratford. The class designation was later made a standard feature for all locomotives on the LNER and 'Class B17' returned in the late 1930s. No. 2813 has an express near Ipswich, around 1938.

Opposite above NO. 2816 – CHORLEYWOOD

Even though the B17s were initially intended for work in the Great Eastern Area, Ipswich shed had a working to Manchester. No. 2802 *Walsingham* was initially allocated to Gorton depot to balance the service, before relieved by no. 2809 *Quidenham*. With the introduction of locomotives just with steam and vacuum brakes, for engine and train respectively, as part of the first batch from Darlington, the decision was made to send the Westinghouse-fitted no. 2809 to the GE Area. The replacement for the engine at Gorton was no. 2816 *Fallodon*, which was the first B17 to establish itself at the depot. As more class members were built and allocated there, the duties became more varied and B17s became increasingly visible on the ex-Great Central main line, working expresses between Manchester and Marylebone. No. 2816 has such a train here at Chorleywood, north west of Rickmansworth, on the Metropolitan & Great Central Joint line on 30th June 1934. No. 2816 would be at Gorton until transferred to Norwich in early 1938.

Opposite below NO. 2817 – WHITTLESFORD

An express from Cambridge is just a short distance to the south of the city at Whittlesford on 25th July 1933. No. 2817 *Ford Castle*, which is in charge of the train, was the first B17 allocated to Cambridge shed when dispatched from Darlington Works in November 1930.

Below NO. 2818 – WHITTLESFORD

A group of children (left) look on in awe as no. 2818 *Wynyard Park* passes by with a southbound express at Whittlesford on 30th July 1934. The locomotive followed classmate no. 2817 to Cambridge shed from Darlington Works within just a few days of completion.

NO. 2819 – WHITTLESFORD

No. 2819 *Welbeck Abbey* is aided by Holden D15 Class 4-4-0 no. 8797 in hauling this express at Whittlesford around 1935; the latter was rebuilt with a round-top boiler in 1937.

Above NO. 2822 – MANNINGTREE

Several boat trains for Holland ran under the LNER, one being the 'Flushing Continental', which is approaching Manningtree station here, behind no. 2822 *Alnwick Castle*.

Below NO. 2823 – ROMFORD

The 'Flushing Continental' appears again, though this time no. 2823 *Lambton Castle* has the train at Romford during August 1931. The engine was new to Colchester but moved to Parkeston in mid-April 1931.

Opposite above **NO. 2826 – ROMFORD**

Just a few months old here near Romford in August 1931, no. 2826 *Brancepath Castle* still has Darlington's green livery on the cylinder sides and 'Class B17' on the bufferbeam. These would be changed when Stratford carried out the first general repair, which took some time, lasting from mid-August to early November 1932. No. 2826 spent much of the decade at Parkeston shed.

Opposite below **NO. 2827 – PARKESTON SHED**

Parkeston shed had several B17s on the roster from the introduction of the class, as the duties there included several heavy boat train services. The engines at the depot could also find work on expresses to Ipswich and elsewhere in East Anglia. No. 2827 *Aske Hall* was new from Darlington in March 1931 and was at Stratford for two-and-a-half years, before a brief stint at Ipswich. From December 1933 to January 1939, no. 2827 was at Parkeston, where the engine stands in the yard, moving on to Cambridge for a long spell in the city.

Below **NO. 2824 – SHEPRETH**

No. 2824 *Lumley Castle* has wandered off the ex-GER London to Cambridge main line and taken the Great Northern route, being captured at Shepreth on 12th August 1944. The latter was originally the terminus for an extension of the Hitchin & Royston Railway, which connected with the GNR main line at the former, and a station opened there in 1851. The Eastern Counties Railway built a connection from the company's line to Cambridge and operated through to Hitchin for a time. Yet, the GNR took over the line in 1866 and started services to Cambridge. No. 2824 has a stopping train for the city and is in the wartime black livery with 'NE' on the tender.

NO. 2829 – CAMBRIDGE STATION

Allocated to Cambridge at the start of 1939, no. 2829 *Naworth Castle* is at the city's station during the year with an express ready to leave for London. Photograph courtesy Rail Photoprints.

Above NO. 2830 – ROMFORD

A London-bound express hauled by no. 2830 *Thoresby Park* speeds through the Romford area in August 1931.

Below NO. 2830 – SHELFORD

No. 2830 *Thoresby Park* approaches Shelford station with a southbound stopping train on 22nd June 1932.

NO. 2830 – IPSWICH

When classmate no. 2870 *Tottenham Hotspur* was transformed to work the new 'East Anglian' train, the name was at first discarded. The club later wanted the locomotive to operate a train and the LNER had to quickly restore the name, with no. 2830 *Thoresby Park* chosen. This engine's name was not reused. No. 2830 *Tottenham Hotspur* is near Ipswich with a London express after the change occurred in January 1938.

Above NO. 2831 – LITTLEBURY

No. 2831 *Serlby Hall* emerges from Littlebury tunnel with a southbound express on 15th June 1931. The engine had been in traffic for just six weeks and was employed at Stratford shed.

Below NO. 2832

No. 2832 *Belvoir Castle* and crew pose at an unidentified shed, likely during the early 1930s. Still visible on the cylinder sides is Darlington's green livery, whilst 'Class B17' appears to be on the bufferbeam. The locomotive was the first of three B17s allocated to Doncaster shed during the early 1930s.

Above NO. 2835 – BANBURY
A duty of Doncaster's B17s was a fish train to Banbury via Tuxford. No. 2835 *Milton* is at the former in late 1933.

Opposite above NO. 2833 – GRANTHAM STATION
No. 2833 *Kimbolton Castle* has come off a train at Grantham station and been to the shed for servicing around 1935.

Opposite below NO. 2834 – NORTHWICK PARK
In the early 1930s, no. 2834 *Hinchingbrooke* was employed on the ex-GCR main line, firstly at Gorton, then for a year at Neasden before returning to Manchester. The locomotive has an express at Northwick Park at the southern end of the line in 1935.

Below NO. 2838 – IPSWICH

The second batch of 15 B17s was completed at Darlington in 1931 with no. 2836 *Harlaxton Manor*. Several months later, the LNER placed an order for six more locomotives and these appeared in early 1933, with no. 2838 *Melton Hall* the second to enter traffic in March. All the B17s built at Darlington up to and including this batch, were sub-classified B17/2 as the springing arrangement was slightly different to the ten NBLC-built locomotives, which were B17/1. Briefly at Doncaster shed, no. 2838 soon moved on to Norwich depot and was there for a lengthy spell. The engine has an express near Ipswich c. 1935.

Above NO. 2836 – STRATFORD

As a consequence of the severe restrictions in the ex-Great Eastern Railway's area of operations, the tenders fitted to the B17s were of a design similar to those coupled to the B12 Class 4-4-0s. Whilst these tenders did not look particularly out of place with that class, the longer wheelbase of the B17s created a sharp contrast. The GER-type tenders had a coal capacity of 4 tons and 3,700 gallons of water could be carried. B17 locomotives were built with and originally coupled to tenders with matching numbers to the running number. No. 2836 *Harlaxton Manor* was therefore paired with tender no. 2836 when completed at Darlington in July 1931 and this lasted the length of the engine's career. The pair is coupled to a motley selection of carriages, including a vintage clerestory vehicle, at Stratford in the early 1930s.

Above NO. 2841 – WILLESDEN GREEN

View east to Lydford Road bridge near Willesden Green station as no. 2841 *Gayton Hall* approaches with the 15.20 express from Marylebone to Manchester on 5th September 1933. This service was established on the ex-Great Central Railway and had a set formation of six carriages, with an extra through coach for Halifax which detached at Penistone. The set consisted of a third brake, third, third open, restaurant first, first and third brake.

Opposite above NO. 2839 – CHADWELL HEATH

Two locomotives were selected to work the new 'East Anglian' train in 1937 and both were renamed. Just as no. 2830 was rechristened, no. 2839 lost the originally bestowed *Rendlesham Hall* and had *Norwich City* nameplates fitted from January 1938. No. 2839 has an express bound for Ipswich at Chadwell Heath (west of Romford) on 29th June 1939. Interestingly, of the engines named after football clubs, none carried Ipswich Town at any time, as the club did not turn professional until 1936 and was only admitted to the football league in 1938.

Opposite below NO. 2840 – WEMBLEY PARK

No. 2840 *Somerleyton Hall* is at Wembley Park with the 15.20 Marylebone to Manchester train on 11th May 1935. The locomotive was built at Darlington in May 1933 and had a short spell at Doncaster shed before moving to Gorton in June. No. 2840 was fleetingly allocated to Neasden, which was located in the Wembley Park area, from September to November 1935, returning to Gorton until October 1938 when reallocated to March.

Opposite above NO. 2845 – LINCOLN STATION

No. 2845 *The Suffolk Regiment* was the first LNER locomotive to be named after an army regiment during a ceremony at Ipswich on 22nd June 1935. The regiment was celebrating the 250th anniversary from the formation and Major General Sir John Ponsonby had the honour of christening the engine. Amongst the representatives for the LNER were Chairman William Whitelaw, Chief General Manager Sir Ralph Wedgwood, and Chief Mechanical Engineer H.N. Gresley. Following the naming, a special service was run to Bury St Edmunds with ex-servicemen in the regiment at the controls, driver E.N. Brown and fireman W.H. Mortimer. No. 2845 is at Lincoln station in the late 1930s with a continental boat train.

Opposite below NO. 2844

At the end of 1933, Darlington Works was again asked to produce more B17s, though only a small number – five. These entered traffic in 1935 and placed in class part three due to small detail differences in the design from earlier engines. In the main, this largely concerned the springing and frames as an amount of frame problems were still being experienced. No. 2844 *Earlham Hall* was the second locomotive from the batch to enter service in May 1935 and settled to work at Norwich shed.

Below NO. 2842 – STRATFORD SHED

No. 2842 *Kilverstone Hall* was the last of the B17/2 engines to be erected at Darlington in May 1933. Allocated to Doncaster briefly, the locomotive subsequently went to Gorton and Neasden before arriving at Cambridge during April 1937. No. 2842 is on the turntable at Stratford shed in the late 1930s.

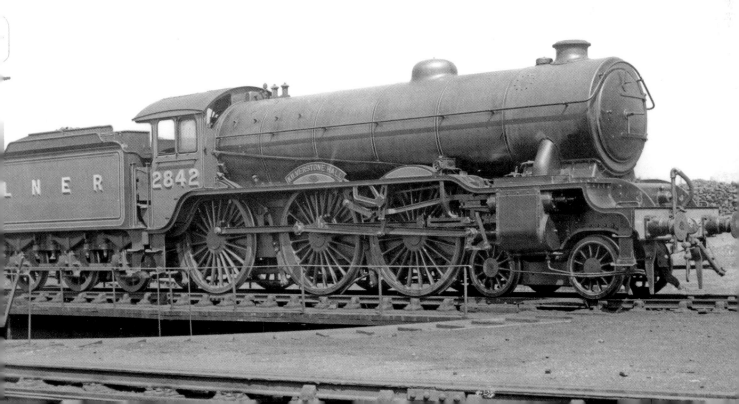

Above NO. 2847 – NOTTINGHAM VICTORIA STATION

With the relatively short notice in naming no. 2845 *The Suffolk Regiment*, those names allotted to the engine and others built subsequently were displaced. No. 2845 was originally to be *Gilwell Park*, no. 2846 *Helmingham Hall* and no. 2847 *Kimberley House*. The latter was ultimately discarded and no. 2847 stuck with *Helmingham Hall* throughout. The locomotive is at Nottingham Victoria station with an express during the late 1930s. As the last B17/3 to traffic in September 1935, no. 2847 was originally paired with GE-style tender no. 2847 which was removed and replaced with Group Standard-type tender no. 2858 from *Newcastle United*; the latter was renamed *The Essex Regiment* soon after. Both engines remained with the same type to withdrawal, though not the tender.

Opposite above NO. 2846 – SPALDING STATION

By the end of the 19th century, a minor railway centre had been formed at Spalding. The town's station dated from 1848 with the opening of the Great Northern Railway line from Peterborough to Doncaster via Boston and Lincoln. The GNR subsequently set about dominating the area, with lines eastward eventually reaching Norwich, Cromer, Lowestoft and King's Lynn. Yet, the company was obliged to form an alliance with the Midland Railway to complete this network and also partnered with the Great Eastern Railway for a line from March to Sleaford, Lincoln and Doncaster. Spalding was connected to these routes and was also particularly important for the local goods traffic, which mainly consisted of tulips. In the LNER period, the station had several platforms and a large goods yard. No. 2846 *Gilwell Park* is with a train at Spalding during the late 1930s; note the highly polished metal work, which is relatively unusual for a B17 in regular service at the time.

Opposite below NO. 2846 – YORK

Starting with no. 2843 *Champion Lodge*, a Wakefield 'Fountain' six-feed lubricator was used to supply oil to the axleboxes, replacing siphon feed from two oilboxes in the cab on the fireman's side. The new lubricator was mounted in the same position and the lines also ran along the right side of the boiler, yet a noticeable bend in the pipes for an air inlet. A feature of the lines peculiar to nos 2843-2847 was the high position they were mounted on the boiler. This is clearly visible on no. 2846 *Gilwell Park*, which is at York on 24th August 1935 when new and perhaps being run in from Darlington Works.

Above NO. 2848 – LEICESTER SHED

Under attention for an issue with the cylinders/motion at Leicester shed on 14th June 1936 is no. 2848 *Arsenal*. The engine had been in traffic for three months and would visit Gorton for light attention in another three.

Below NO. 2848

No. 2848 *Arsenal* poses for the official photograph when new in March 1936.

Above NO. 2850
Completed at Darlington in March 1936, no. 2850 *Grimsby Town* was allocated to Leicester shed by the end of the month.

Below NO. 2851 – NEEPSEND
No. 2851 *Derby County* has a Manchester express at Neepsend, Sheffield, in 1936. Photograph courtesy Rail Photoprints.

Above and below NO. 2853

When completed at Darlington in April 1936, no. 2853 *Huddersfield Town* was one of the latest B17/4s to join the growing number of class members at Leicester Central shed. The locomotives had been drafted in to replace ex-GCR Atlantics on the principal expresses between London and Manchester.

Opposite NO. 2852 – LEICESTER CENTRAL SHED

No. 2852 *Darlington* is in the shed yard at Leicester Central depot on 10th April 1937. Servicing facilities were established on the east side of the station in 1899 and remained in use until the mid-1960s.

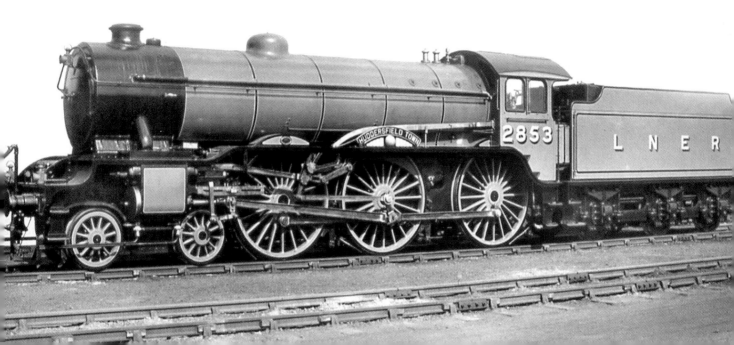

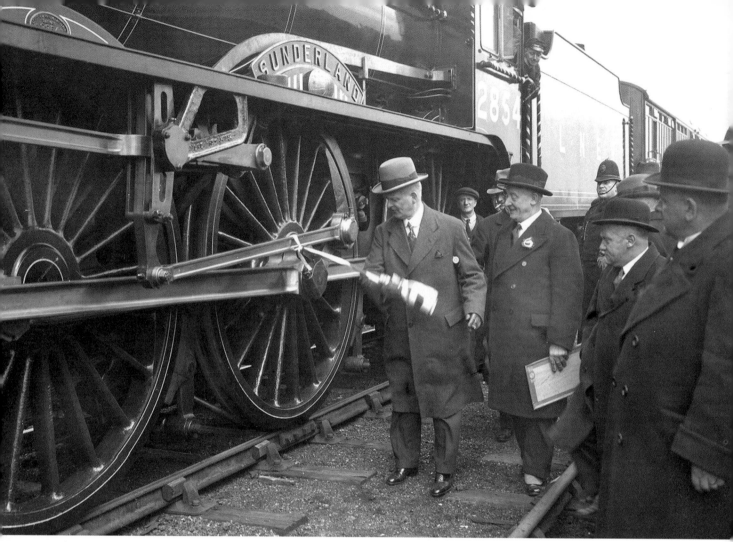

Above **NO. 2854**

When a further 14 B17s were ordered from Darlington in March 1935, the LNER decided to discontinue the naming policy previously adopted. The company turned to football and selected a number of clubs from the LNER's jurisdiction. No. 2854 left Darlington Works in April 1936 and on the 18th was named *Sunderland* during a ceremony. The Chairman of the club, Sir Walter Raine, had the honour of breaking a bottle of champagne against the connecting rods before the team played a match against Huddersfield Town. Sunderland triumphed 4-3 in the game and won the First Division (for the sixth time) in the process.

Opposite above **NO. 2854 – YORK STATION**

No. 2854 *Sunderland* was required to work a special train from Sunderland to Wembley on 1st May 1937 as the team had reached the FA Cup final. Yet, the engine was in Gorton Works and too far along in a general repair to be employed. The nameplates and number were taken from the locomotive and briefly carried by no. 2851 Derby County which worked the special in no. 2854's place. The substitute engine is seen here at York on Cup Final day. The original engine missed out on Sunderland's 3-1 victory over Preston North End, as the team lifted the trophy for the first time. Sunderland did not reach another final until 1973 when upsetting favourites Leeds United.

Opposite below **NO. 2856 – NEASDEN SHED**

No. 2856 *Leeds United* is at Neasden shed, likely during the first year in traffic when allocated there. The engine is still rather presentable, suggesting a date close to when new in May 1936. The B17/4s named after football clubs had individually coloured nameplates representing those of the club. For *Leeds United* these were blue and gold, which recently had been adopted by the club to replace the original blue and white striped shirts.

NO. 2857 – NEASDEN SHED

When new in service, no. 2857 *Doncaster Rovers* was allocated to Neasden shed and the engine is pictured there during the late 1930s. Interestingly, the locomotive never worked from Doncaster depot and did not visit the works until early 1953.

NO. 2858 – IPSWICH

After just a month in traffic, no. 2858 *Newcastle United* was called to Stratford Works for a change in tender, with no. 2847 *Helmingham Hall* providing a GE-type. At the same time, a name change also occured and no. 2858 became *The Essex Regiment*, with *Newcastle United* discarded and not reused. The locomotive has a mixed train in the Ipswich area in the late 1930s.

Above **NO. 2859**

Originally set to be *Sheffield United*, no. 2859 was completed at Darlington Works in June 1936 as *Norwich City*. The engine first worked from Gorton, Manchester, though in September 1937 was transferred to Norwich, by which time no. 2859 had been completely transformed and renamed. This broadside view of no. 2859 has been taken at an unidentified location during the first year in service. No. 2839 was given the *Norwich City* nameplates in January 1938.

Opposite above **NO. 2859 – DONCASTER WORKS**

The mid-1930s was a particularly successful and noteworthy period for the LNER, following the struggles of the depression years at the start of the decade. Chief Mechanical Engineer H.N. Gresley (knighted 1936) had produced the much-publicised P2 Class 2-8-2 locomotives, which were the largest and most powerful passenger engines in the country at the time, and the streamlined A4 Class Pacifics. These extremely striking locomotives were performing unprecedented feats of endurance by working high-speed services for long distances. The success of the 'Silver Jubilee', which was the first service to utilise the A4s, soon encouraged the LNER to introduce more high-speed trains – the 'Coronation' and 'West Riding Limited' – as well as improving other services across the system. One example of this was the 'East Anglian' train and the LNER chose to retrofit A4-style streamlining on two B17 Class 4-6-0s. This was done at Doncaster Works in mid-1937 and no. 2859 *East Anglian* is there outside the weigh house following the transformation.

Opposite below **NO. 2859 – DONCASTER WORKS**

For the most part, the streamlining used on the B17s was the same as the A4 Class. Although, in order to retain the original insulation around the boiler, the streamline casing was fixed over the original clothing bands. The front of the cab was modified to resemble the v-shape of the A4s, whilst the tender had plating added to make a streamlined appearance. The original lubricator for the axleboxes was removed and replaced by a Wakefield type which was located on the right-hand side above the rear coupled wheel in the same position as on the A4s. Following experience with the latter class, longer buffers and drawhook were fitted as the original types were too short due to the overhang created by the wedge front. A chime whistle also replaced the standard LNER single note example. No. 2859 *East Anglian* is in the Crimpsall Repair Shop, Doncaster Works, coming to the end of the transformation on 19th September 1937.

Above NO. 2860 – NOTTINGHAM VICTORIA STATION

The fireman is in the tender of no. 2860 *Hull City* and manoeuvring the hose from the water column into the tank. The LNER group standard tender provided to the B17/4s had a much greater capacity from the restricted GE-type. Some 4,200 gallons of water and 7 tons 10 cwt of coal could be carried in the tender, which was also paired with a number of other classes. No. 2860 is at Nottingham Victoria station with an express in the late 1930s.

Opposite NO. 2859 – BELSTEAD

As part of the celebrations for the coronation of George VI in 1937 and the general push by the LNER for new, improved services, the 'East Anglian' train was introduced for the winter timetable. This was a Liverpool Street to Norwich express, with a stop at Ipswich, which left the capital at 18.40 for arrival at 20.55. The southbound service departed from Norwich at 11.55 and terminated in London at 14.10. A new set of carriages was assembled for the train and these included a third class brake, kitchen first, open first, open third, kitchen third and third brake. In relation to the 'Silver Jubilee', the 'Coronation' and 'West Riding Limited' expresses, the 'East Anglian' required a lower average speed in 50 mph range, compared to the A4-hauled services in the high 60s. No. 2859 *East Anglian* has a southbound 'East Anglian' train at Belstead during the late 1930s.

Below NO 2861 – SPALDING STATION

One of Gresley's personal crusades during the 1920s and 1930s was to induce either the LNER or Government to provide a locomotive testing station. This would allow designs to be evaluated before being put into production, as well as researching the steam locomotive for further development. Just before the war, Gresley was successful in persuading W.A. Stanier of the London Midland & Scottish Railway to pool the two companies' resources to build a facility at Rugby. Unfortunately, the war intervened in construction and Gresley sadly died in 1941. The project did proceed after the conflict ended and A4 Class Pacific no. 60007 *Sir Nigel Gresley* was the first locomotive to demonstrate the station's capabilities when opened in 1948. Without the aid of a dedicated testing station, locomotives had to run on the main line, with several disadvantages to achieving reliable data. Nevertheless, tests were often conducted and information was gathered on B17 performance in the mid-1930s. No. 2861 *Sheffield Wednesday* was the locomotive selected for trials which took place in the North Eastern Area using the dynamometer car and a counter pressure locomotive. The latter was Worsdell B13 Class no. 761 and the engine provided resistance, which could be varied, for the locomotive under test. Over four days, no. 2861 ran on the straight and level section of track north of Thirsk, travelling at various speeds and cut-offs. The engine was found to produce around 1,400 horsepower at relatively long cut off (45%), though at short cut off no. 2861 was found to be underpowered at high speed, suggesting a flaw in the design of the cylinder ports. Further data was spoiled by problems encountered during subsequent days' testing and no. 2861 returned to traffic; *Sheffield Wednesday* has an express at Spalding station in the late 1930s.

Above NO. 2862 – WELWYN GARDEN CITY

A final order for 11 B17 Class locomotives was placed in February 1936 at Robert Stephenson & Co., with these entering service in 1937. No. 2862 *Manchester United* was the first of the batch to be completed and dispatched in January 1937. The engine was new to Gorton shed and worked there for over two years before transferring to Cambridge shed. No. 2862 has an express from the city bound for King's Cross station at Welwyn Garden City on 8th April 1939.

Above NO. 2866 – DARLINGTON

Posing proudly at the Robert Stephenson & Co. Works, Darlington, are an engineman and no. 2866 *Nottingham Forest*. The final 14 B17s built by the company were overseen by nearby Darlington Works and as a result these locomotives received painted cylinder sides and 'Class B17' on the bufferbeam. A feature unique to the engines was the all-welded tender, whilst Darlington had used riveting for all previous B17s. The difference was identifiable at the top of the tender, as welded ones had flush sides at this point, whereas riveted examples had a step between the two pieces.

Opposite above NO. 2863 – SWINDON SHED

Nos 2863 *Everton*, 2864 *Liverpool* and 2865 *Leicester City* were allocated from new to Sheffield (Neepsend) shed. These locomotives were put to work on the cross country Swindon to York train, with an engine taking charge from Leicester to Swindon, then working the return as far as Sheffield. In a demonstration of friendly rivalry, these engines were always worked hard over the Great Western Railway section and no. 2863 was particularly noted for achieving high speeds away from Swindon. On one occasion, Driver C.H. Skelton was recorded taking the train to Didcot, 20 miles from Swindon, in 17 minutes 30 seconds or a minute faster than the GWR's 'Cheltenham Flyer', which was one of the company's top services, and *Everton* almost reached 90 mph. No. 2863 is in the shed yard at Swindon for servicing during 1937. The Sheffield engines were all transferred away in January 1938.

Opposite below NO. 2864 – CHORLEYWOOD

The 15.20 Marylebone to Manchester express is at Chorleywood in 1938, with no. 2864 *Liverpool* leading the train. Following the spell at Sheffield, the locomotive was reallocated to Gorton depot and was there for eight years. No. 2864 continued to be employed on the ex-GCR main line until 1951, including spells at Colwick, Annesley and Woodford, then moving to the ex-GER section.

Above NO. 2870 – DARLINGTON

No. 2871 was to be named *Tottenham Hotspur* when completed by Robert Stephenson & Co. in mid-1937. A special ceremony for christening the engine was planned for 29th May at an exhibition of rolling stock at Walthamstow, yet as the date approached no. 2871 was not ready. No. 2870 *Manchester City* had been completed in mid-May and was being run-in when recalled. The locomotive was duly renamed *Tottenham Hotspur* and is in works grey livery here at Robert Stephenson & Co. Works, Darlington, following the change. At the exhibition, the Chairman of Tottenham Hotspur, Mr Charles Roberts, named no. 2870.

Opposite above NO. 2870 – DONCASTER WORKS

No. 2870 *Tottenham Hotspur* was only in traffic (allocated to Leicester) for just over a month before admitted to Doncaster Works for rebuilding with streamline casing. The transformation took around two months and no. 2870 emerged with another new name, *City of London*, which was deemed more appropriate and representative of the area served by the new 'East Anglian' train. No. 2870 is almost ready to be dispatched from Doncaster here and is in the Crimpsall Repair Shop in early September.

Opposite below NO. 2870 – IPSWICH

Whilst several railway companies around the globe had introduced streamlining in the 1930s, many did so for publicity rather than design purposes. Gresley was interested in the latter and research had been carried out at the National Physical Laboratory on behalf of the LNER and LMSR by F.C. Johansen into the wind resistance of locomotives. He found that at 60 mph the wind resistance accounted for a third of the total resistance of the train and the locomotive required 346 horsepower to overcome this. Further, a good proportion of the fuel cost was lost to overcoming the drag created by the air. Gresley also believed that streamlining would allow faster running uphill and this would promote a greater saving in time and fuel as a reduced horsepower would be necessary to take the train up the acclivity. A further benefit to be derived from streamlining was moving exhaust smoke away from the cab, which had been a problem highlighted at the time, and Gresley had a model of the A4 in a wind tunnel to determine the best shape for this. No. 2870 *City of London* provides a demonstration of this latter point at Halifax Junction water troughs, just south of Ipswich, in the late 1930s. There were two sets of troughs on the GER main line, with the other at Tivetshall St Mary near Norwich.

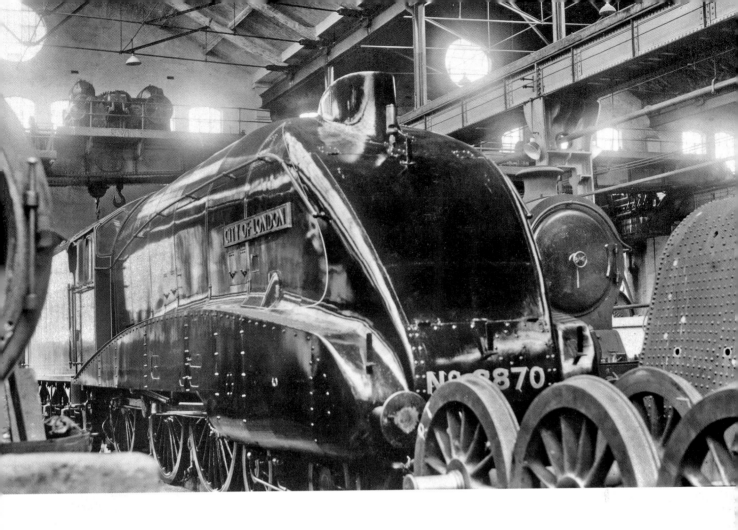

Above NO. 2871

Manchester City was reused when no. 2871 was completed in mid-June 1937. The engine was allocated to Gorton from new until May 1939 when transferred to Leicester. No. 2871 is in an unidentified depot yard in the late 1930s.

Below NO. 2872

No. 2872 *West Ham United* has an unidentified Pullman train in late July 1937 shortly after being constructed.

Above NO. 1603 – STRATFORD SHED

Rebuilt in October 1946, no. 1603 *Framlingham* is in the yard at Stratford shed during 1947. The locomotive has acquired North Eastern-style tender no. 8663 from C7 Class Atlantic no. 737.

Below NO. 1603 – COLCHESTER NORTH SHED

Around Nationalisation, no. 1603 *Framlingham* is outside Colchester North shed. Photograph courtesy Rail-Online.

Above NO. 1617 – GREENWOOD

What might be considered an orderly approach to numbering was not considered a priority by many railway companies. The constituents of the LNER tended to fill in gaps between classes, or those left by withdrawn locomotives. At Grouping, the LNER inherited around 7,000 locomotives and, even though the class designation system was relatively orderly, the numbering continued to be erratic, as the original number tended to be retained with a digit added to the start depending on which area the engine worked in. Sir Nigel Gresley's successor Edward Thompson decided to recast the LNER's numbering system in 1943. In this, he gave precedence to the principal express engines, such as the Pacifics, followed by 4-6-0s, etc, with groups of 1,000 numbers dedicated to them. The B17s fell into the second category and were grouped into nos 1600-1672, which was applied to the engines, as well as those being rebuilt to B2 specifications, starting January 1946 and taking a year. No. 1617 *Ford Castle* was renumbered, likely at Cambridge shed, in early February 1946 and has a train from the city to King's Cross at Greenwood (near New Barnet) during the spring of 1946. The locomotive was soon to become a B2 Class engine, with the process taking six months at Darlington Works, beginning in June.

Below NO. 1610 – KIRBY CROSS STATION

Even though the GER reached Colchester by 1843, some time was taken to make extensions that connected to the coast at Clacton-on-Sea and Walton-on-the-Naze. The latter was reached first in May 1867, as the culmination of several sections being finished over the previous years, with Kirby Cross station open to traffic from Colchester in July 1866. Clacton-on-Sea had to wait until 1882 for the rail connection to be completed. Both lines had been constructed by independent companies and operated by the GER, though the lines were amalgamated by the end of the century. No. 1610 *Honingham Hall* has a local train at Kirby Cross station in 1949. Photograph courtesy Rail-Online.

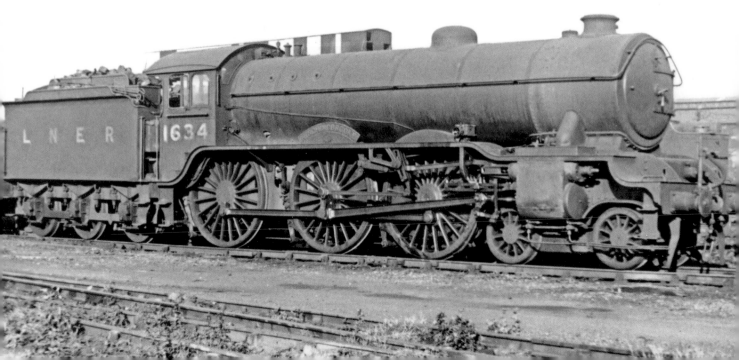

Above NO. 1637 – WALTON-ON-THE-NAZE

From November 1941, all LNER engines were painted black for economy reasons and a year later 'LNER' was no longer applied to the tender, rather 'NE'. This practice continued for a period after the end of the war and, whilst some engines, such as the Pacifics, quickly returned to LNER green, many B17s saw in Nationalisation still with wartime black. No. 1637 *Thorpe Hall* was no exception and the locomotive has an added layer of grime over the black; 'LNER' appears to have been restored at some point only to be lost again. The locomotive has a service at Walton-on-the-Naze station during early 1948 as BR no. 61637 would be in use from September. Photograph courtesy Rail-Online.

Opposite above NO. 1635 – MARCH SHED

After leaving Doncaster shed for Norwich in April 1938, no. 2835 *Milton* had just two further allocations. In March 1940, the locomotive began a two-year spell at Stratford, leaving for March depot in April 1942. The engine is pictured in the shed yard, with the building, along with War Department 'Austerity' 2-8-0 no. 63013, in the background, during 1949. No. 2835 became no. 1635 in September 1946. Photograph courtesy Rail-Online.

Opposite below NO. 1634 – STRATFORD SHED

Out of service at Stratford shed and waiting for works attention in June 1947 is no. 1634 *Hinchingbrooke*. The engine was noted as receiving light attention, yet the visit lasted three months, suggesting a backlog of repairs or lack of materials at the shops. No. 1634 had been a month at Stratford for another light repair at the end of 1946 and was the first time the locomotive returned to the works since 1934. As *Hinchingbrooke* was mainly allocated to the ex-GC section during the 1930s, Gorton had responsibility for maintenance and this even continued when the engine moved to the GE section after the outbreak of war. Two visits were even paid to Darlington Works in 1945 and 1946.

Above **NO. 1655 – STRATFORD SHED**

As a number of B17s were displaced from the GC Section following the introduction of Gresley's V2 Class 2-6-2s there were plans to send the aforementioned to Scotland. This did not happen and the engines were allocated to sheds in England, yet authority given to fit a number of these with Westinghouse equipment was upheld, no doubt as the equipment was still necessary for those moved to the GE Section. No. 1655 *Middlesbrough* was one engine equipped during a general repair at Gorton in December 1941. The locomotive is pictured here at Stratford shed in August 1947 following a general repair at the works. 'LNER' has been reapplied to the tender and a fresh coat of black covers no. 1655. The number was changed in November 1946.

Opposite above **NO. E1664 – GRANTHAM**

Just as the LNER did not have a scheme in place for numbering the absorbed locomotives at Grouping, British Railways was in the same position at Nationalisation. For a brief period, letter prefixes were added to some locomotives depending on the Region they were at work in. Eastern Region engines were given an 'E' and no. E1664 *Liverpool* had the prefix applied during a general repair at Stratford in February 1948. The scheme was only short-lived and BR decided to add 60,000 to the original number for ex-LNER engines. E1664 *Liverpool* carried the prefix for some time until the BR number was used from March 1950. Another feature briefly implemented was the application of 'British Railways' to the tender. In some cases, as here, the lettering was distinctly smaller than the numbering on the cabside – 10 in. compared to 12 in. E1664 *Liverpool* is at Grantham during 1949.

Opposite below **NO. 1668**

No. 1668 *Bradford City* was another engine to be fitted with Westinghouse brake equipment in early 1941. The locomotive has an express from Liverpool Street at an unidentified location in mid-1947.

Above NO. 1671

The Royal Family has a long standing connection with the railways. As early as 1840, the Great Western Railway constructed a special coach for Queen Victoria to travel in and subsequently several companies constructed dedicated train formations for Royal personages to be conveyed to various points within certain company's systems, as well as others. With the monarch having palaces and places of residence across the country, travel in some areas was quite frequent, causing companies to designate a particular engine to serve with the Royal Train. The Great Eastern Railway operated trains to Wolferton station, Sandringham, for a succession of monarchs, beginning with Edward VII, and latterly used 'Claud Hamilton' 4-4-0s. In LNER days, no. 8783 and no. 8787 were specially selected and based at Cambridge to work Royal Trains, with a regular driver accompanying them. After the war, a new engine was chosen to take the place of the aforementioned pair, no. 1671 *Manchester City*, which recently had been rebuilt to B2 Class specifications. At the same time a name change occurred and no. 1671 became *Royal Sovereign*. The engine is leaving London with an early evening King's Cross to Cambridge local train in around 1947.

Below **NO. 1671 – KING'S CROSS STATION**
After being rebuilt in August 1945, no. 2871 *Manchester City* moved to Cambridge shed. The engine was renumbered 1671 in February 1946 during a repair at Stratford, also being repainted LNER green, then in April was rechristened *Royal Sovereign*, becoming the main Royal engine at Cambridge, although the 'Claud Hamiltons' previously used were often coupled to the Royal train from King's Lynn to Wolferton. As such, the locomotive was kept on specific duties, such as the morning Cambridge to Liverpool Street train and return, as well as the afternoon Cambridge to King's Cross service. No. 1671 is at King's Cross station in 1947.

Above NO. 61600 – MOUNTNESSING

Even though there was standardisation of components on the LNER, Edward Thompson wanted to take this further and implement more sweeping measures. When the B17 Class required replacement boilers, his diagram 100A boiler, which had been developed from the diagram 100 originally fitted to the class, was selected. The main feature of these was the increase in working pressure to 225 lb per sq. in. against the 200 lb per sq. in. used hitherto. Consequently, affected engines were reclassified B17/6. No. 61600 *Sandringham* was altered to carry the new boiler in mid-1950. The locomotive has an express bound for Liverpool Street a short distance north east of Brentwood at Mountnessing on 14th September 1951.

Below NO. 61600 – STRATFORD SHED

Between duties at Stratford shed on 26th June 1955 is no. 61600 *Sandringham*. The locomotive was allocated to the depot at the time, with this lasting from February 1953 to January 1957, when transferring to Cambridge for six months. No. 61600 returned and was withdrawn from Stratford in July 1958. Doncaster Works scrapped the engine soon after. Photograph by Bill Reed.

Above NO. 61603 – SOUTHEND-ON-SEA (VICTORIA)

The London, Tilbury & Southend Railway had been established for well over 30 years before the Great Eastern Railway implemented plans to build a competing line to Southend and Southminster. The new route left the main line at Shenfield, then split at Wickham to Southend-on-Sea and Southminster. The GER line served the area north of the LT&SR and arrived at Southend from that direction. The station, originally named Southend-on-Sea, was open from October 1889 and had been designed by the GER architect W.N. Ashbee. He planned all the stations on the line using the 'domestic revival' architectural style, which embraced traditional English functional features. The station subsequently underwent several name changes, becoming Southend-on-Sea (Victoria) following Nationalisation. No. 61603 *Framlingham* arrives at the station with a train from Shenfield on 18 April 1954. Photograph courtesy Rail-Online.

Opposite above NO. 61601

Whilst 57 B17s ultimately carried the diagram 100A boiler, six retained the original type throughout their lives. No. 61601 *Holkham* was one of these locomotives and remained relatively unchanged throughout. One difference from new is the tender as no. 2801 was removed in September 1948 and changed to no. 2802, which was used until withdrawn in January 1958; the aforementioned was coupled to no. 2805. No. 61601 *Holkham* is at an unidentified location in the early 1950s, with Holden J15 Class 0-6-0 no. 65448 on the left.

Opposite below NO. 61602 – YARMOUTH SOUTH TOWN SHED

The East Suffolk Railway opened a line from Ipswich to Yarmouth in mid-1859, establishing South Town station. At this time a small engine shed was built south of the facility, on the east side of the line. This building survived amidst increasing dereliction until rebuilding in 1956, only to be closed three years later and torn down. No. 61602 *Walsingham* is there for servicing in August 1957. Photograph by Bill Reed.

Above NO. 61604 – DONCASTER WORKS

In 1953, Doncaster Works celebrated 100 years from the opening of the shops. These had been established in the town thanks to MP Edmund Denison, who was also Chairman of the Great Northern Railway. He had been Doncaster's saviour during the planning stages of the line, as the original intention was to travel via Gainsborough to Selby and bypass Doncaster altogether. The town subsequently became very important on the railway and the works produced a number of world-renowned locomotives, such as Ivatt C2 Class Atlantic no. 990 *Henry Oakley*, which was to run a special train alongside Ivatt C1 Class Atlantic no. 251 as part of the centenary celebrations. Sadly, no. 61604 *Elveden* was not to be part of the large open day held over the weekend of 19th/20th September 1953 (attracting well over 30,000 visitors) or working another special train. The locomotive was at Doncaster Works – pictured outside the Paint Shop with no. 990 on 30th August – for scrapping, following 25 years in service. The first B17 had been withdrawn a year earlier and no. 61604 was the second in 1953; the next would not occur until 1958. This small number of withdrawals is unexplained, though could relate to the large number of new BR Standard Class 7 'Britannia' Pacifics taking over the B17's services in the GE Section. Photograph by Geoff Warnes.

Below NO. 61603 – ARDLEIGH

No. 2803 *Framlingham* was rebuilt at Darlington to B2 specifications in October 1946 and was renumbered 1603 at the same time. The locomotive was Ipswich-based at this point, though at the end of the year a move to Parkeston occurred. Just two months later no. 1603 was transferred again to Colchester, where *Framlingham* was allowed to settle. Receiving the BR number in January 1949, no. 61603 is just north of home base at Ardleigh in October 1955 with an up freight, which is worked in partnership with an unidentified Gresley K3 Class 2-6-0. *Framlingham* moved to Cambridge in November 1956 and was condemned there in September 1958. Photograph courtesy Rail-Online.

Above **NO. 61606 – MOUNTNESSING**

No. 61606 *Audley End* has a southbound express at Mountnessing on 14th September 1951. Recently fitted with a diagram 100A boiler at a general repair carried out at Stratford, the locomotive was also a resident of the shed there. No. 61606 had arrived in June 1946 and had ten years at Stratford before moving on to Colchester. Withdrawal occurred at the depot in September 1958.

Opposite below **NO. 61605 – DONCASTER WORKS**

No. 2805 *Burnham Thorpe* carried the name of the Earl of Leicester's residence near Hunstanton for ten years from new. Then, in 1938, the engine became the second class member to take the name of an army regiment. On 4th May, a ceremony was organised at Lincoln station for no. 2805 to be christened *The Lincolnshire Regiment* by Major General C.R. Simpson. Upon naming the locomotive he commented: 'This engine now becomes affiliated with the Lincolnshire Regiment. We wish it a long life in the ranks of the London & North Eastern Railway, serving the country as we soldiers serve it in another way'. *The Lincolnshire Regiment* was in traffic for a total of 30 years, mainly working from Stratford shed. The engine is at Doncaster Works on 12th November 1955 following a general repair. Photograph by Bill Reed.

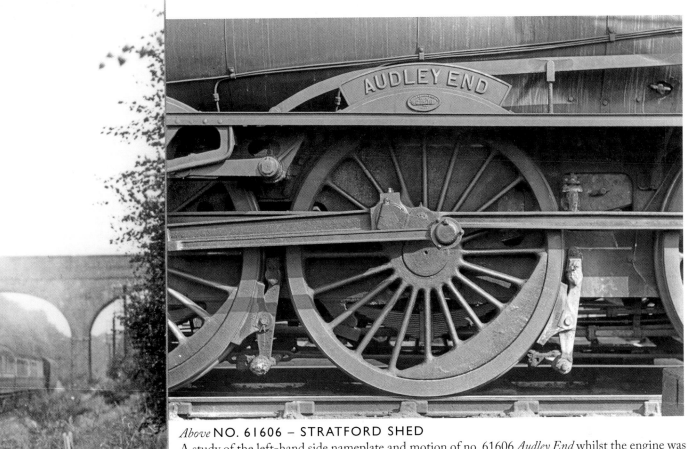

Above **NO. 61606 – STRATFORD SHED**

A study of the left-hand side nameplate and motion of no. 61606 *Audley End* whilst the engine was resting at Stratford shed on 18th May 1957. The style of nameplate varied over the construction of the class. The NBLC cast the plates in brass with 'Sans Serif' lettering and beading on just three sides. As mentioned previously, originally the company placed the nameplates on the leading splasher and was told to move them to the centre on the first few engines. The nameplate then fouled the reversing rod, causing the splasher to be widened by 4 in. and this continued to be the case until 1935. The plate below the name reads: 'London & North Eastern Railway 61606 built 1928'. This has been modified as the original number – no. 2806 – has been covered over by a strip of metal bearing the BR number.

Above and opposite NO. 61607 – LIVERPOOL STREET STATION

Edward Thompson had radical plans to reshape the LNER's locomotive fleet when he took the position of Chief Mechanical Engineer. These mainly called for the reduction in the number of classes and their replacement by several standard types. The number of 4-6-0 classes was to be culled dramatically and replaced by new B1 4-6-0s and rebuilt classes from existing locomotives. The B17s were to have a cylinder removed and the new diagram 100A boiler fitted. Initial authorisation was given for 20 conversions and no. 2871 *Manchester City* was the first in 1945. Nine more followed up to 1949, but several changes in circumstances halted the programme. No. 61607 *Blickling* was the penultimate rebuild, with the work carried out at Darlington in May 1947. The engine is on the turntable in these two images taken at Liverpool Street station in mid-1958. Both photographs by Bill Reed.

Above NO. 61608 – STRATFORD SHED

Under preparation for the next duty as Stratford shed around 1958 is no. 61608 *Gunton*. Good quality coal is in the tender, which was no. 2800. This had been attached in early 1950 and remained with the engine to the end, whilst original tender no. 2808 was coupled to no. 61612 *Houghton Hall* soon after. A quantity of coal can be seen to have spilled over the sides of the coal space and this was a problem noted from the introduction of the class. The coal guard on the right side, which was where the fireman stored the fire irons (in the space between the coping plate), had been raised by 8 in. to reduce the amount slipping over. Stratford shed was located a short distance away from Stratford station and the first depot was established in 1840 and was adjacent to the works. This was later absorbed into the shops and a new building was erected just to the west. Extra space was soon required and a 12-track shed was built in 1887 and no. 61608 is outside this structure here. Photograph by Bill Reed.

Opposite NO. 61610 – MARCH SHED

Just as Spalding was a hub for several lines in the area, so too was March, which was a short distance to the south. Connections were made with Spalding, Wisbech, Cambridge, Huntingdon and Peterborough. By the turn of the century, several goods yards had been established at March, mainly for the transfer of coal, but also seasonal goods and produce. The LNER built a vast marshalling yard, Whitemoor, to handle this traffic in the 1920s and also improved stabling facilities. The first B17s had arrived at March shed in the early 1930s and were used on passenger services in the area. As time progressed, more B17s were allocated and at Nationalisation nine were at the shed. No. 61610 *Honingham Hall* was primarily a Stratford engine and only arrived at March in May 1958, spending 18 months there. Photograph by Bill Reed.

NO. 61611 – STRATFORD STATION

View north east from the down main platform at Stratford station on 10th April 1958. No. 61611 Raynham Hall is passing through with a Yarmouth South Town, via Beccles and Ipswich, to Liverpool Street express. Photograph by B.W.L. Brooksbank.

Above NO. 61612 – MARKS TEY STATION

An express has stopped at Marks Tey station during June 1950, with no. 61612 *Houghton Hall* leading. In BR green livery, the locomotive has a non-standard red background to the nameplate. Photograph courtesy Colour-Rail.

Below NO. 61612 – NORWICH SHED

In Norwich shed's yard during July 1959 is no. 61612 *Houghton Hall*. Just two months remained for the engine.

Above **NO. 61614 – KING'S CROSS STATION**

No. 61614 *Castle Hedingham* was rebuilt to B2 specifications in June 1946. A distinguishing feature of several of these locomotives was the coupling of ex-North Eastern Railway C7 Class Atlantic tenders. Originally, the intension was to fit group standard tanks to the frames of these, but the amount of work necessary caused the adoption of the tender without change. The water capacity was similar at 4,125 gallons, though a smaller amount of coal could be carried – 5½ tons compared to 7 tons 10 cwt. No. 61614 received tender no. 8641 from C7 no. 718 and this had curved coal rails when the pairing was made. A change occurred in mid-1957, where the rails were altered for a GE-type stepped coping plate that differed by curving at the rear. Allocated to Cambridge from October 1956, no. 61614 *Castle Hedingham* is at King's Cross, likely with a service for the city in the late 1950s. Photograph courtesy Rail-Online.

Opposite above and below **NO. 61610/61613 – DONCASTER WORKS**

Traditionally, scrapping withdrawn locomotives was carried out at the operating company's workshops. This was so certain components could be retained and reused. By the end of steam in the early to mid-1960s, private companies played a greater role in the process due to the sheer volume of engines out of service, as well as the retention of parts becoming redundant. In the late 1950s when the B17s were meeting their end, BR's workshops still had the capacity to deal with locomotives ready for disposal and the cutters are making short work of this group at Doncaster Works in early 1960. The carcass of a Thompson Pacific is in the foreground and is likely an A2/2, as two – no. 60503 *Lord President* and no. 60505 *Thane of Fife* – were the only locomotives of that type at Doncaster in this period. Behind is a pair of B17s: no. 61613 *Woodbastwick Hall* and no. 61610 *Honingham Hall*. Both engines had been condemned at Cambridge shed in late 1959 and just short of 30 years in service. Doncaster Works scrapped 51 of the B17s, whilst Stratford dealt with the remainder and the B2 Class.

Above NO. 61616 – MARCH SHED

No. 61616 *Fallodon* is at March shed during the late 1950s. *Fallodon* was allocated to Cambridge shed and this was the third spell there over 30 years in traffic. On the left is LNER-built DES1 diesel electric shunter no. 15000. This locomotive had been at March from 1945 to work in the marshalling yard, alongside the other three members of the class; several other unidentified diesel shunters are visible here. Photograph by Bill Reed.

Opposite above NO. 61616 – LIVERPOOL STREET STATION

View from Pindar Street bridge to the platforms at Liverpool Street station on 4th October 1948. Below is no. 61616 *Fallodon* which is light engine and looks to be ready to work a passenger service. Rebuilt to join the B2 Class in November 1945, the engine was paired with tender no. 8648 from C7 no. 733. At this time *Fallodon* still had the original number and was painted unlined black with 'NE' on the tender. Renumbered 1616 in August 1946, the locomotive now has 'British Railways' applied, which is the larger 12 in. type, though is still in black livery, as LNER green did not return to use on the majority of B2s until 1949. Interestingly, whereas other express classes had BR blue applied for a time, the B2s had LNER green until BR dark green was adopted around 1952. This view of no. 61616 also shows the revised method of attaching the nameplates. With the splashers now shallower than on the B17s, the support ribs on the back had to be milled off and brackets created for the plates to be bolted on to the running plate. Photograph by B.W.L. Brooksbank.

Opposite below NO. 61615 – BETHNAL GREEN

Whilst the majority of B2 rebuilds received NER-type tenders from withdrawn C7s, the recent scrapping of Gresley's P1 Class 2-8-2 locomotives in 1945 released two tenders for use with class members. These had a water capacity of 4,700 gallons and 7 tons of coal. The C7 tenders were little modified before coupling, but the P1 type required quite a lot of frame work due to boosters being originally fitted to the P1s. No. 61615 *Culford Hall*, which was rebuilt in April 1946, took tender no. 5293 from no. 2393 and used this through to withdrawal. The locomotive is at Bethnal Green station on 30th August 1958 with the 12.14 express from Liverpool Street to Hunstanton – due there at 15.54. Photograph by B.W.L. Brooksbank.

NO. 61618 – BECCLES STATION

A relief express from Yarmouth to Liverpool Street has made a stop at Beccles station during the late 1950s. No. 61618 *Wynyard Park* is the engine taking a rest. Photograph courtesy Colour-Rail.

Above NO. 61617 – LITTLEBURY

Twelve miles south of Cambridge at Littlebury, no. 61617 *Ford Castle* has an express for Liverpool Street station on 15th August 1953. No. 61617 was the first B2 Class locomotive to be taken out of service in August 1958.

Below NO. 61619 – CAMBRIDGE STATION

No. 61619 *Welbeck Abbey* is with a local service at Cambridge in 1953. Photograph courtesy Rail Photoprints.

Above NO. 61620 – SHEFFIELD VICTORIA STATION

A good number of B17s were coupled to the same tender throughout their lives. One was no. 61620 *Clumber* which ran with no. 2820 from new in November 1930 until condemned during January 1960. Interestingly, the second BR emblem applied to the tender side is facing the wrong way, as the grant of arms from the College of Heralds was for the lion to face the left. Several classes of locomotive displayed this mistake until corrected. The locomotive is at Sheffield Victoria station on 6th September 1958 and was allocated to March shed. Photograph by Geoff Warnes.

Opposite NO. 61619 – NEW SOUTHGATE

No. 61619 *Welbeck Abbey* travels northward at New Southgate with a stopping train on 30th August 1948. The engine had recently emerged from Stratford Works following a light repair and the BR number was applied at this time. A modified Gill Sans style was used, where the tails of the 6 and 9 curled round and only a small number of locomotives were treated in this way.

Above NO. 61622 – LIVERPOOL STREET STATION

During the war, the boilers of the B17s had the working pressure reduced from 200 lb per sq. in. to 180 lb per sq. in. As no. 2822, *Alnwick Castle* had this change implemented in October 1943. Three years later, the engine was fitted with a diagram 100A boiler, though the working pressure remained at 180 lb per sq. in. A short time later, no. 1622 was selected to perform trials against B2 no. 1607 *Blickling* and the pressure was raised to 225 lb per sq. in., which was 5 lb higher than the standard for the boiler. In the tests, with a 13-coach train between Liverpool Street and Norwich, the B17 was found to be generally superior, if rough-riding. No. 61622 is at Liverpool Street station with an express on 15th August 1957. Photograph by D.J. Dippie.

Opposite above NO. 61620 – CHALONER'S WHIN JUNCTION

No. 61620 *Clumber* has an express c. 1955. The locomotive is at Chaloner's Whin Junction, just south of York. This was the point where the original York & North Midland Railway line to Leeds joined the North Eastern Railway's 1871 route to Selby and Doncaster. Photograph courtesy Colour-Rail.

Opposite below NO. 61621 – WORKSOP STATION

In the BR period, B17s at Parkeston generally worked the boat train to Sheffield as far as March, where a classmate from the depot there took over. No. 61621 *Hatfield House* has an eastbound service at Worksop station on 24th May 1958. The locomotive had been at March shed from January 1954 and was condemned there in November 1958. This was the third spell at March, with the first occurring between June 1935 and January 1939 and the second from June 1951 to June 1953. Photograph by Geoff Warnes.

Above **NO. 61623 – POTTERS BAR**

The line northbound from King's Cross was not particularly favourable for locomotives, especially with heavy trains. At Hornsey, three miles from the terminus, the line began to rise at 1 in 200 and continued at this gradient for another nine miles to Potters Bar. No. 61623 *Lambton Castle* has reached this point with a train – consisting of Gresley stock decorated in BR's carmine and cream livery – bound for Cambridge in 1951. Photograph courtesy Colour-Rail.

Opposite above **NO. 61625**

Built at Darlington in February 1931, no. 61625 *Raby Castle* spent most of nearly 30 years in service working in East Anglia. The locomotive was delivered new to Ipswich and had ten years there before transferred to Norwich. Two switches were made between these two depots, then at Nationalisation a move to Cambridge occurred. Returning to Ipswich in June 1953, no. 61625 had two months at Cambridge before condemned in December 1959. *Raby Castle* is pictured at an unidentified location in 1956. The locomotive did not carry a diagram 100A boiler. Photograph courtesy Rail Photoprints.

Opposite below **NO. 61623 – DONCASTER WORKS**

The cutting gang take a short break at Doncaster Works to happily pose for the camera. No. 61623 *Lambton Castle* is in the process of being torn apart during late summer 1959 after withdrawal at the end of July. The engine had been a long-term resident at Cambridge following a transfer there in October 1945.

Below NO. 61626 – WICKER, SHEFFIELD

The Sheffield, Ashton-under-Lyne & Manchester Railway terminated at a station north east of Sheffield city centre at Bridgehouses when opened in December 1845. Plans were formulated soon after to connect the route to Grimsby. Two companies were formed to do this, though both were quickly amalgamated with the SA&MR to form the Manchester, Sheffield & Lincolnshire Railway. One Act was authorised for the construction of a section of the route between Sheffield and Gainsborough. Part of this task included the erection of a viaduct to carry the line from Bridgehouses over the Wicker, River Don and Sheffield Canal. The structure was 660 yards long and featured a 72-ft span to allow the Wicker thoroughfare to pass through, with 30 ft of headroom. No. 61626 *Brancepath Castle* passes over the viaduct during the late 1950s. In the background, on the right side, Wicker goods station can be glimpsed. This was the site of the terminus for the Sheffield & Rotherham Railway which became a goods depot following the opening of Sheffield Midland station in 1870.

Above NO. 61627

Fifty-seven B17s were fitted with a diagram 100A boiler. This was developed from the boiler originally used with the class and was quite similar, though the main difference was the working pressure raised to 225 lb per sq. in. and thicker plates were used to withstand this. The firebox was slightly longer by an inch, being 9 ft at the bottom, and the front tubeplate was shortened by a small amount. The number of small tubes was also reduced by two and this slightly lowered the overall heating surface of the diagram 100A boiler. An external difference was the addition of a fifth washout plug at the firebox end. No. 61627 *Aske Hall* was equipped with a new boiler in November 1948, although this was with the lower pressure setting and an out of course visit was made to Darlington for the change to 225 lb per sq. in. to be made. The locomotive has a train of empty coaching stock at an unidentified location, c. 1955; note the Great Central Railway trespass warning sign on the extreme left.

NO. 61628 – DONCASTER WORKS
The first B17 to be condemned was no. 61628 *Harewood House* in September 1952. The engine is pictured at Doncaster Works a short time later waiting to be scrapped. Photograph courtesy Colour-Rail.

Above NO. 61627 – MARCH SHED

No. 61627 *Aske Hall* is at March shed during 1957. The locomotive had been allocated there from June 1954 and was condemned at the depot in July 1959.

Below NO. 61627

At an unidentified location with a local passenger service is no. 61627 *Aske Hall*. Photograph by Malcolm Crawley.

Above **NO. 61630 – DONCASTER STATION**

No. 61630 *Tottenham Hotspur* had a large number of allocations over 27 years in service. In the 1930s, the engine was either at Stratford or Parkeston, with six months at Gorton, whilst the early 1940s was similar, though with a spell at March covering the second half of the decade. The allocation still had a year left to run when the locomotive was pictured with a southbound express at Doncaster during April 1951 and no. 61630 returned to Stratford. Periods at Cambridge and March punctuated longer stays at Stratford up to withdrawal in August 1958. Photograph by Geoffrey Oates.

Opposite **NO. 61629 – LIVERPOOL STREET STATION**

Whilst the B17s had performed admirably within tight restrictions and in a trouble-free manner (apart from some frame issues and complaints of rough riding), the Great Eastern main line passenger services were scheduled for improvement by BR in the early 1950s. For this, BR allocated a large number of new Standard Class 7 'Britannia' Pacifics to the region when introduced in 1951. Many schedules were improved and frequency increased. The fastest trains to leave Liverpool Street were timed at 76 minutes to Ipswich with a greater number of carriages than before. Therefore, the B17s had to take a supporting role in East Anglia, with Thompson B1 4-6-0s also squeezing the class out. No. 61629 *Naworth Castle* managed to keep employment at Norwich and Ipswich under BR before withdrawn in September 1959. The locomotive is in the servicing area at Liverpool Street station during the latter part of the decade with 'Britannia' no. 70010 *Owen Glendower* behind. Photograph by Bill Reed.

Above NO. 61631 – WITHAM

Between Chelmsford and Colchester, no. 61631 *Serlby Hall* has an express at Witham on 31st May 1956. After the first 15 locomotives took their names from country houses in East Anglia, the choice for following locomotives was extended to those further afield in LNER territory. *Serlby Hall* was taken from the home of Viscount Galway near Retford, Nottinghamshire. Originally no. 2831, the locomotive became no. 1631 in September 1946 and used the 'E' prefix between March and October 1948 when taking the BR number. At the time of this picture, *Serlby Hall* was still in original condition, though in October 1957 a diagram 100A boiler was fitted. Withdrawal occurred 18 months later in April 1959.

Below NO. 61632 – STRATFORD SHED

No. 61632 *Belvoir Castle* appears to have been a recent visitor to Stratford Works and is in the shed yard here during the mid-1950s. Under BR, the locomotive was allocated to Colchester, then moved to Cambridge in October 1956. Two years later, when no. 61671 *Royal Sovereign* was withdrawn, the decision was taken to perpetuate the name and the plates were taken from the latter and given to no. 61632. The locomotive ran with the new name for just a short time, as withdrawal occurred in February 1959. Photograph courtesy Rail-Online.

Above **NO. 61634 – DONCASTER WORKS**

Fresh from a general repair in the early 1950s, no. 61634 *Hinchingbrooke* is steamed at Doncaster Works ready to return to traffic. Stratford and Gorton Works originally shared maintenance duties for the B17 Class, depending on which section the engine was allocated, although there were exceptions. From 1943, Darlington took responsibility for those in Stratford's jurisdiction and this role soon extended to those working elsewhere. Before Nationalisation, the situation reverted to the original arrangement, yet soon after Darlington was again repairing engines that should have been at Stratford Works. Gorton Works had sole responsibility for the class between mid-1949 and late 1951, when Doncaster Works took over and the B17s visited there for repair until withdrawn. No. 61634 first visited Doncaster for a general repair in 1950 and ran around 18 months and two years between visits subsequently. The *Locomotives of the LNER Part 2B: Tender Engines – Classes B1 to B19* records that no. 61634 had the highest mileage recorded to the last general repair in early 1957, which also saw the engine receive a diagram 100A boiler. By this time no. 61634 had exceeded 1,000,000 miles and was one of the few class members to do so. Photograph by Malcolm Crawley.

Opposite **NO. 61633 – MARCH SHED**

When nos 2800-2809 were erected, the NBLC omitted front footsteps and only provided one footstep at the cab end. These features were later added to the aforementioned engines, as well as new class members; another provision was a handrail on the face of the cab. No. 61633 *Kimbolton Castle* had these features from new in May 1931, though the engine was completed just a short time before the hinged sight screen was provided between the two cab windows and this was fitted at a later date. The locomotive is at March shed during the late 1950s. Allocated there from November 1956, withdrawal occurred at the depot in September 1959. Photograph by Bill Reed.

Above NO. 61636 – LITTLEBURY

No. 61636 *Harlaxton Manor* is at Littlebury in late summer 1952 with the Saturday non-stop service to Cambridge. The locomotive was a recent addition to the ranks at the city's depot and was engaged there until June 1958 when transferred to Norwich. Withdrawal from there occurred in October 1959.

Below NO. 61635 – DONCASTER WORKS

At Doncaster Works for an unrecorded visit in April 1957 is no. 61635 *Milton*; attention appears to be centred on the motion as the connecting rod is missing. The smokebox door to the diagram 100A boiler (first fitted at Darlington in January 1949) is open and part of the blastpipe and chimney liner can be seen. The arrangement of these had taken some time to be satisfactorily set. Originally, the NBLC engines had a 5¼ in. diameter blastpipe top that sat some 3½ in. below the centre line. Steaming troubles ensued soon after, resulting in a reduction of the blastpipe diameter to 5 in. and lowering the top by just over 2 in. Although affecting an improvement, Stratford Works introduced a new design for the blastpipe which mixed the exhaust thoroughly before reaching the top and opened the orifice out to 5⅛ in. The top was also lowered to 8¼ in. below the centre line. The design of the blastpipe top was altered in 1934 and all combined to produce the arrangement employed through to the 1950s. In the middle of this decade the liner and cowl were changed to combat steaming troubles brought on by a decline in the quality of coal. The new setting was applied to 27 engines before discontinued as the class was withdrawn. Photograph by Bill Reed.

NO. 61638 – SHEFFIELD VICTORIA STATION

An express service headed by no. 61638 *Melton Hall* is at Sheffield Victoria station c. 1955. Photograph courtesy Colour-Rail.

Above NO. 61637 – CAMBRIDGE STATION

The driver of no. 61637 *Thorpe Hall* inspects his engine, whilst the water supply in the tender is replenished at Cambridge station on 17th September 1951. Original tender no. 2837 had been replaced by no. 2834 just after Nationalisation. Photograph by Geoffrey Oates.

Below NO. 61638 – DONCASTER WORKS

Two visits were made by no. 61638 *Melton Hall* to Doncaster Works in 1954 for an issue to be adressed. The first occurred in April, then the engine returned in June. Photograph courtesy Rail Photoprints.

Above NO. 61639 – MARCH SHED

No. 2839 *Norwich City* entered Darlington Works in May 1945 for rebuilding as a B2. The engine emerged six months later and was ultimately the only 'footballer' in the class. *Norwich City* was renumbered 1639 in May 1946 and later had the 'E' prefix for nearly two years before the BR number was in use. At some point after rebuilding, the locomotive's nameplates had the colours reversed. As built the yellow panel was next to the football, with green on the outside, whereas the opposite was the case subsequently. No. 61639 is at March shed during the 1950s. Photograph courtesy Rail-Online.

Opposite above NO. 61640 – ARDLEIGH

No. 61640 *Somerleyton Hall* is near Ardleigh with an express on 9th October 1955. Earlier in the year, the locomotive had been fitted with a diagram 100A boiler. Photograph courtesy Rail-Online.

Opposite below NO. 61640 – CAMBRIDGE

Just north of Cambridge station at Newmarket Road on 14th August 1954, no. 61640 *Somerleyton Hall* approaches with a down express. The engine was a long-term servant at Cambridge shed and had arrived in January 1947, remaining until condemned in November 1958. No. 61640 had been at the depot on two previous occasions, the first from November 1938 to January 1939 and the second was between August 1941 and May 1944. *Somerleyton Hall* had originally worked on the ex-GCR main line and also had periods based at Norwich, Stratford and Parkeston. Photograph courtesy Rail-Online.

NO. 61641 – STRATFORD SHED

Next to the turntable at Stratford shed in the late 1950s is no. 61641 *Gayton Hall*. Photograph by Bill Reed.

Above NO. 61641 – YARMOUTH VAUXHALL STATION

In August 1957, no. 61641 *Gayton Hall* departs Yarmouth Vauxhall with an express. Photograph by Bill Reed.

Below NO. 61642 – DONCASTER WORKS

No. 61642 *Kilverstone Hall* is at Doncaster Works for a general repair in the early 1950s. The first carried out there was in November 1951 and a further three took place before scrapped on site during late 1958. There were also three out of course visits and the engine also attended Stratford in March 1953 for similar attention. Photograph by Malcolm Crawley.

Above **NO. 61642 – BROXBOURNE**

Between Harlow and Cheshunt at Broxbourne with a train for Cambridge on 23rd July 1955 is no. 61642 *Kilverstone Hall*. The locomotive had been a long term resident at the city, being allocated from April 1937 until withdrawn in September 1958. No. 61642 received a diagram 100A boiler in January 1949.

Opposite above **NO. 61643 – ORGREAVES COLLIERY JUNCTION**

A Sheffield-bound express passes Orgreaves Colliery signal box, which controlled the colliery line to the left, on 16th April 1955. No. 61643 *Champion Lodge* is the locomotive leading the train. March-allocated at this time, withdrawal from the depot occurred in July 1958. Photograph by Geoff Warnes.

Opposite below **NO. 61643 – DONCASTER STATION**

No. 61643 *Champion Lodge* is at the southern bay platform at Doncaster station with a local service ready to depart in the early 1950s. The engine is yet to be rebuilt with a diagram 100A boiler, which took place at the town's works in October 1954. Doncaster had taken over maintenance duties from a general repair that was carried out between October and December 1952. A total of seven visits were made before the final one for disposal.

NO. 61644 –
HAVERHILL STATION
At Haverhill station – on the
Cambridge to Colchester line
– with a freight service on 19th
October 1959 is no. 61644 *Earlham
Hall*. The locomotive was nearly
a month away from withdrawal.
Photograph courtesy Colour-Rail.

NO. 61644 – STRATFORD SHED

The last B17 rebuilt to B2 was no. 61644 *Earlham Hall* in March 1949. At Stratford shed in the late 1950s, the locomotive was also one of just two class members fitted with Westinghouse brakes, though the other – no. 61607 *Blickling* – was equipped from new and no. 61644 had the pump added when rebuilt. Photograph by Bill Reed.

Above NO. 61647 – DONCASTER WORKS

No. 61647 *Helmingham Hall* is in the yard at Doncaster Works on 12th April 1953 after completing the first general repair there. The engine is standing next to the Weigh House, which was an important place at the works, as determining the correct axle loads was vital for the trouble-free running of the locomotive. The building was arranged with a pit - 58 ft long and 4 ft deep - running almost the full length, bordered by a pair of rails, and containing the weighing equipment. There were 14 separate devices forming the weighing machine, seven being placed on each side, and these had a capacity of 12 tons. The weighing units worked on the steelyard system where two arms, one short (supporting the weight of the object) and the other long arm (resting on a pivot) are out of balance until a weight on the latter brought the pair into balance. With the arrangement at Doncaster, the steelyards were connected to each other which allowed the actual weight of the locomotive to be determined, in addition to the weight supported on each unit being displayed. When each individual unit was balanced, the springs were adjusted to carry the right weight by turning the nuts on the screwed spring links either tight or loose. With the weight distribution correct the locomotive rested evenly and level on the springs. When in traffic this allowed the power to be transmitted smoothly and the riding was relatively free from disturbance. The springs used by the first ten B17s were the standard laminated type, consisting of nine plates, 5 in. wide and ⅝ in. thick. Following the high number of frame issues suffered, this arrangement was changed to fifteen ½ in.-wide plates. The axle load was different between the various class parts, but was generally around 18 tons. Photograph by Malcolm Crawley.

Opposite above NO. 61645 – IPSWICH STATION

The 11.01 express from Gorleston-on-Sea to Liverpool Street via Lowestoft rushes through Ipswich station on 7th July 1951. No. 61645 *The Suffolk Regiment* is at the head of the train. Allocated to the latter town's shed at this time, the engine had several moves during the 1950s, visiting Stratford, Colchester, Cambridge and March depots. Photograph by B.W.L. Brooksbank.

Opposite below NO. 61646 – MARCH SHED

The first shed was established at March by the Eastern Counties Railway in 1850 a short time after the opening of the Ely to Peterborough line. This building was originally at the station, yet when the marshalling yards were established to the north west, the facilities were moved there. The new shed was built from brick and contained six lines, opening in 1884. In the mid-1920s the LNER added further stabling space on to the north of the GER building. No. 61646 *Gilwell Park* is in the shed yard during the late 1940s. Photograph courtesy Rail-Online.

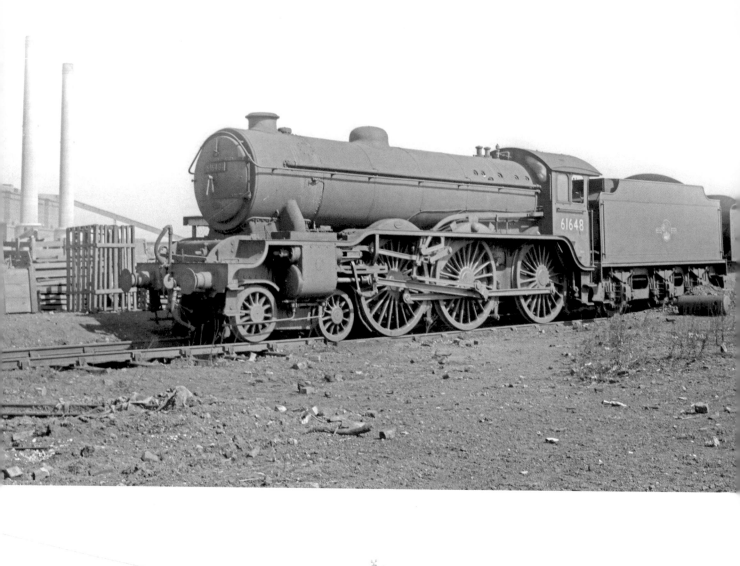

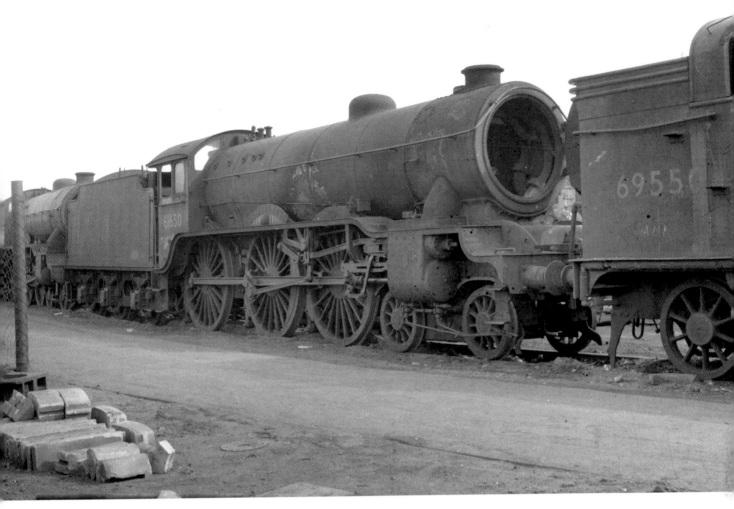

Above **NO. 61650 – DONCASTER WORKS**

A pair of B17s is at Doncaster Works for scrapping in early 1959. No. 61650 *Grimsby Town* stands closest to camera, whilst the other is unidentified and Gresley N2 Class 0-6-2T no. 69550 is also on the scrap line. No. 61650 worked on the ex-GCR main line for much of the time in service, though from May 1951 the engine was allocated to Stratford, then two years later moved on to Colchester. Withdrawal from there occurred in September 1958. Photograph by Bill Reed.

Opposite above **NO. 61648 – DONCASTER WORKS**

No. 61648 *Arsenal* waits to be scrapped at Doncaster Works in early 1959. The nameplate and shedplate have been removed, though the football, smokebox numberplate and works plate remain on the engine. The method of securing the nameplate is revealed and was different to the 'Sandringham' engines. The plates were cast flat and fixed to a rear support, rather than using integral ribs. The football was attached to the face of the splasher and was made with a long threaded bolt. Many of the nameplates were later gifted to their respective clubs and no. 61648's was displayed at Highbury for many years. Photograph by Bill Reed.

Opposite below **NO. 61649 – DONCASTER WORKS**

No. 61649 *Sheffield United* is at Doncaster Works in the spring of 1952 on the occasion of the engine's first general repair there. On the following visit, nearly two years later, a diagram 100A boiler was fitted. After this, the locomotive only returned on three other occasions before being condemned in February 1959 and brought back to the site for scrapping. Apart from a month at Yarmouth in late 1949, *Sheffield United* spent the BR period allocated to Ipswich shed. Photograph courtesy Rail-Online.

Above **NO. 61651 – STRATFORD SHED**

At Stratford shed in 1953 is no. 61651 *Derby County*. The locomotive is yet to receive a diagram 100A boiler but this was soon fitted at Doncaster Works in June. By the end of the year, no. 61651 was taken off the roster at Stratford following two years there and was then employed at Colchester. *Derby County* had six months at Cambridge before withdrawn in August 1959. Photograph courtesy Rail-Online.

Opposite above **NO. 61653 – CHADWELL HEATH**

In the mid-1950s, no. 61653 *Huddersfield Town* pollutes the air at Chadwell Heath whilst working an express. The locomotive has a diagram 100A boiler, placing the image after May 1954 when the change occurred at Doncaster. No. 61653 was Cambridge-allocated from late 1950 until November 1957 when transferred to March. Photograph from the John Day Collection courtesy Rail Photoprints.

Opposite below **NO. 61652 – HORNSEY STATION**

No. 61652 *Darlington* is with an express at Hornsey station in the late 1950s. The engine was allocated for most of the decade at Cambridge shed and was withdrawn there in September 1959; Doncaster Works, perhaps gladly, disposed of the locomotive. Photograph courtesy Rail-Online.

Above NO. 61654 – HYTHE STATION

A local train from Walton-on-the-Naze arrives at Hythe station (south east of Colchester) in the mid-1950s. No. 61654 *Sunderland* is leading the short train and was allocated to the town's depot at the time. This lasted from June 1953 to October 1955 when departing for Stratford. In June 1958, the locomotive transferred to Norwich and was withdrawn there in November 1959. Photograph courtesy Rail-Online.

Opposite NO. 61653 – SPALDING STATION

No. 61653 *Huddersfield Town* is at Spalding station in 1958 with a local train. The engine mostly had been employed on the ex-GCR section until December 1950 when arriving at Cambridge. These allocations included stints at Doncaster, Leicester, Sheffield, Gorton and Colwick. Spalding was a busy point for the railways in the area into the early BR period. Towards the end of the 1950s, a decline set in and the line to Bourne and King's Lynn was closed in 1959, whilst the route to Boston ceased to carry traffic in 1970. The line from March managed to hang on to the 1980s thanks to freight traffic. Now only the line from Peterborough and to Sleaford is active. Photograph courtesy Colour-Rail.

Above NO. 61656 – LIVERPOOL STREET STATION

In April 1958 no. 61656 *Leeds United* arrives at Liverpool Street station with an express, passing 'Britannia' Pacific no. 70003 *John Bunyan*. Photograph courtesy Colour-Rail.

Opposite NO. 61655 – DONCASTER WORKS

No. 61655 *Middlesbrough* is in the yard of the Crimpsall Repair Shops, Doncaster Works, in the spring of 1959. The locomotive was condemned in April and cut up on site; no. 61655 appears, from rust accumulated on the wheels, to have been out of service for a period. Photograph by Bill Reed.

Above **NO. 61658 – STRATFORD SHED**
Tender no. 2847 of the GE-type was paired with no. 61658 *The Essex Regiment* from renaming in 1936 until February 1946. At this time, a swap with no. 2846 *Gilwell Park* occurred and the tender from this engine was carried through to no. 61658's demise in December 1959. The tenders for nos 2843-2847 had vacuum brakes from new and originally the reservoir cylinder was mounted underneath the dragbox. From the mid-1930s, this was repositioned to the rear of the tender between the coal space and filling cap for the water tank. In this respect, the tender conformed to the Group Standard tenders fitted to subsequent engines and the reservoirs on both types were 4 ft 6 in. long, with a diameter of 1 ft 10 in. No. 61658 is at Stratford shed during the late 1950s. Photograph by Bill Reed.

Opposite above **NO. 61657 – DONCASTER WORKS**
Coppersmith Bill Thorpe is working on no. 61657 *Doncaster Rovers* next to the Crimpsall Repair Shops in the late 1950s. With March depot's '31B' code on the smokebox door, the date is narrowed down to one between March 1956 and withdrawal in June 1960. There were four visits over this period: three casual in 1956, 1957 and 1959; one general repair in 1958. The locomotive is likely in for light attention and the work undertaken here has involved removing the motion. Interestingly, no. 61657 was not scrapped at Doncaster, as Stratford was given the task. Photograph by David Thorpe.

Opposite below **NO. 61657 – BETHNAL GREEN STATION**
In common with several other stations in London, Liverpool Street promised a difficult start for trains leaving. Particularly, from East London Junction to Bethnal Green, the line rose at a 1 in 70 gradient. No. 61657 *Doncaster Rovers* has successfully overcome this obstacle on 30th August 1958 and reached Bethnal Green station with an express for Caister-on-Sea, near Great Yarmouth, where there was a holiday camp. Photograph by B.W.L. Brooksbank.

Above NO. 61659 – LIVERPOOL STREET STATION

During 1948, no. 61659 *East Anglian* is with a train at Liverpool Street station. The date is after April 1948 when Stratford Works sent the engine back into traffic following a general repair. This comprised applying a fresh coat of wartime black livery, as well as the BR number and 'British Railways' on the tender. The latter was the small-style 10 in. transfers which contrasted against the 12 in. number on the cabside. The font of both numbers on the cab and front is the modified Gill Sans style with curved tails to the 6 and 9. *East Anglian* only remained with these features for a year when entering Darlington Works for another general repair. LNER green was applied at this time, though not as when first streamlined. For an unexplained reason, the black at the front end did not finish with a curve before the nameplate, rather the colour extended past this to the first clothing band. Only a small number of early green A4s had this style in the mid-1930s as there were concerns the green would not withstand high temperatures in the smokebox, yet no instances of trouble with no. 4482 *Golden Eagle*, which had the same livery as no. 2859 as new, or the two streamlined B17s appears to have been recorded. Another feature of interest in this image is the standard LNER whistle carried by no. 61659 in place of the chime type. These were removed from most of the locomotives so fitted as the company thought there was a similarity to the sound of air raid sirens used in the war and confusion could be caused between the two. Photograph courtesy Rail-Online.

Opposite NO. 61659 – LIVERPOOL STREET STATION

The first alterations made to the streamlined casing of no. 2859 and 2870 occurred early in the Second World War when the skirting over the wheels was discarded to aid maintenance. No. 2859 differed at first by returning to traffic with the casing still in place ahead of the cylinders, which was in keeping with A4 Class no. 4462 *William Whitelaw* as the first class member altered; on both, this piece was soon removed by shed staff. Another anomaly on no. 2859 was a piece of curved metal plating behind the cylinder – mirroring the one in front – was omitted and the space between the latter and the running plate was left at a right angle. In late 1950, the decision was made to remove the casing from both B17s and no. 61659 was transformed at Gorton between November and April 1951. *East Anglian* also lost the straight nameplates at this time and received a pair of curved plates in the traditional position. No. 61659 has an express at Liverpool Street station in the late 1950s. Photograph by Bill Reed.

Above NO. 61660 – WELLINGBOROUGH

No. 61660 *Hull City* was only a month away from withdrawal when caught with the crew at Wellingborough on 30th April 1960. March-allocated at this time, the locomotive had been there for just a few months, arriving from Lowestoft earlier in the year. Previously, no. 61660 had a long-term allocation at March, this lasting from November 1942 to June 1951, with allocations to Stratford book-ending this period. *Hull City* was one of the few B17s to retain the diagram 100 boiler type throughout, whilst the engine was also in the minority converted to Westinghouse brakes in February 1940. Photograph courtesy Rail-Online.

Opposite above NO. 61660 – SHEFFIELD VICTORIA STATION

The 'North Country Continental' had origins stretching back to the 1880s as the Great Eastern Railway exploited the company's control of east coast ports providing connections to Europe. When introduced in the middle of the decade, the service was amongst the first long-distance cross-country trains and pioneered restaurant services, later taking another first with the use of a third class dining car. The destination of the service was Parkeston, with carriages from York, Manchester, Liverpool and Birmingham forming the train. In this direction, the train was an early evening departure from these places, whilst in the opposite direction, an early start was made. Here, at Sheffield Victoria station on 28th July 1950, the eastbound train has no. 61660 *Hull City* at the head. The departure from Liverpool had been made at 13.15, travelling to Manchester Central and reaching Sheffield via Woodhead. Arrival at Parkeston was scheduled for 21.15 as the train travelled via Retford, Lincoln, March and Ipswich. Photograph by B.W.L. Brooksbank.

Opposite below NO. 61660 – LIVERPOOL STREET STATION

Stratford shed was a distance away from Liverpool Street station making travel to and from the depot problematic given the volume of traffic in and out of the station. Therefore, servicing facilities were provided at several points, meaning engines needing a quick turnaround could be dealt with on site. The station's turntable was located between Pindar Street and Primrose Street – carried on bridges over the running lines – and the track visible on the bottom left connected with the servicing area adjacent to the cab road off Pindar Street. No. 61660 *Hull City* is on the apparatus during 1955. Photograph courtesy Rail Photoprints.

Above NO. 61661 – LIVERPOOL STREET STATION

View from the platform at Liverpool Street station to the servicing yard next to the cab road off Pindar Street bridge on 14th December 1949. No. 61661 *Sheffield Wednesday* is under attention after working an unidentified service. The engine is now in BR green with 'British Railways' on the tender in the larger lettering which matches the size of the number on the cabside. At a general repair undertaken by Darlington in August 1949, the livery had been applied and a tender change had taken place. For four years previously, no. 2865 had been coupled, but the engine's original tender, no. 2861, was re-coupled and remained with no. 61661 until withdrawal. A detail of the tender was the number plate, which can be glimpsed here below the top lamp iron and next to the highest footstep. This was 8¾ in. by 5 in. and featured the works of construction and the date. Pre-no. 2837, a different style had been used and this was 5½ in. by 3 in. and had just the number. Photograph courtesy Colour-Rail.

Opposite NO. 61661 – MARYLEBONE STATION

Following Nationalisation, BR chose locomotives from several classes to model potential new liveries and these engines were exhibited at several locations. No. 61661 *Sheffield Wednesday* was one ex-LNER locomotive that was transformed in 1948. Interestingly, no. 61661 was painted at Doncaster Works in a light green livery with yellow lining and fitted with a front smokebox numberplate. Subsequently, the engine was displayed at Marylebone station, but the livery was quickly found unacceptable and returned to Doncaster for the lining to be changed to white, yellow and red with the same green. After a spell standing at King's Cross for inspection, no. 61661 returned to traffic at Yarmouth and worked a specially painted train, with a chocolate and cream livery also under consideration, to Liverpool Street. No. 61661 ran in the livery for about a year before being one of the first B17s to take BR dark green livery with orange and black lining. *Sheffield Wednesday* is at Marylebone station with the first livery in April 1948; note the club's colours have been lost on the splasher. Photograph courtesy Colour-Rail.

Above **NO. 61663**

As no. 2863, *Everton* was the third 'footballer' to be fitted with Westinghouse brake equipment. The engine had been in the ex-GE Section from late 1938 after leaving Doncaster for Stratford. The equipment was fitted at the latter place's works, whilst at the next visit to shops, which occurred at Gorton nearly three years later in mid-1943, the boiler pressure was reduced to 180 lb per sq. in. The same works also fitted a diagram 100A boiler in November 1951. No. 61663 *Everton* is pictured at an unidentified location in the mid-1950s working an express. The locomotive was Stratford-allocated at this time, moving to Colchester in December 1958 and returned to Stratford in November 1959 for three months before condemned. Photograph courtesy Rail Photoprints.

Opposite above **NO. 61662 – COLCHESTER**

In store at Colchester in February 1959 is no. 61662 *Manchester United*. The locomotive had been allocated to the town's depot from December 1953 and only had a month away at Stratford before withdrawal in December 1959. Also in store is Holden J19 Class 0-6-0 no. 64647, which had been at the depot for much of the BR period and the engine returned to service the following month at March before withdrawal during early 1960. Photograph courtesy Rail Photoprints.

Opposite below **NO. 61662 – DONCASTER WORKS**

No. 61662 *Manchester United*'s first visit to works after entering traffic from Robert Stephenson & Co. in January 1937 was to Doncaster in April of that year for light attention. Allocated to Gorton at this time, the engine had possibly experienced a failure on the road and had to go to the nearest shops. No. 61662 did not return to Doncaster for attention until 1953 when the locomotive's eighth general repair took place. Nearly two years later, the next general occurred and *Manchester United* was fitted with a diagram 100A boiler. The engine was noted as returning a further two times, for a non-classified repair and a final full overhaul in December 1956, before condemned. No. 61662 is on the scrap line in early 1960, with a good start made by the cutting gang on dismantling the locomotive.

Above **NO. 61664**

In the late 1940s to early 1950s, no. 61664 *Liverpool* is at an unidentified location on the ex-GCR main line with a local service. A Woodford Halse shed plate is on the smokebox door and this only lasted from June 1949 to May 1951, at which time the engine moved to ex-GE lines. No. 61664 had been on the Great Central Section from new, with spells at Sheffield, Gorton, Leicester, Colwick and Annesley. The locomotive had a significant number of moves in the 1950s, but these were mostly between Norwich and Yarmouth. *Liverpool* was briefly at Lowestoft and March before withdrawal in June 1960. Photograph courtesy Rail-Online.

Opposite above **NO. 61666 – LONG MELFORD STATION**

Whilst various forms of transport – private cars, buses, trams, etc – had vied with the railways for passengers from the early 20th century, after the Second World War the competition became increasingly fierce, especially from cars and buses. In the early 1950s, British Railways had a market share of 21.4% of the passenger traffic and, importantly, 45% of freight was moved on the rail (most of the 'big four' companies relied on transporting goods to make money). Yet, by the middle of the decade these figures had fallen, respectively, nearly 3% and 5% and at the end of the decade were 6% and 16% lower. This was particularly disastrous for BR and the company was haemorrhaging money at an alarming rate. The Modernisation Plan of 1955 was an attempt to stem the losses, though unfavourable political forces made the case terminal. As an older class, the B17s were amongst the earliest of the ex-LNER withdrawals in the late 1950s, meaning that the subsequent preservation movement was unable to save any class members. No. 61666 *Nottingham Forest* managed to survive until March 1960 as one of the few B17s left in service and was in the minority to be scrapped at Stratford. The locomotive is at Long Melford station – on the line between Colchester and Bury St Edmunds – with a local service in July 1959. Photograph courtesy Colour-Rail.

Opposite below **NO. 61666 – STOKE STATION**

Stoke station (in Suffolk) was opened by the Great Eastern Railway on 9th August 1865 on the final section of the Stour Valley Railway. The first part had traffic running in 1849 and left the main line to Colchester, Ipswich, etc, at Marks Tey, heading northward to Sudbury. Later, the line was extended to Haverhill, with a branch to Bury St Edmunds, meeting a branch leaving the Cambridge main line at Shelford. No. 61666 *Nottingham Forest* is at Stoke station, which was just east of Haverhill, with a local train on 19th October 1959. Stoke station was a victim of the 'Beeching axe' in 1967, along with the line between Shelford and Sudbury, though trains still run between the latter and Marks Tey. Photograph courtesy Colour-Rail.

Above **NO. 61667 – BARNBY DUN**

No. 61667 *Bradford* has a train of empty wagons at Barnby Dun (north east of Doncaster) on 16th April 1954. Eight days previously, the locomotive had undergone a general repair at Doncaster Works and was perhaps being run in here. The home base for no. 61667 was Colwick shed (east of Nottingham) and this was the case until September 1957 when transferred to Stratford. The engine had a month at Cambridge before withdrawal in June 1958. Photograph by Geoff Warnes.

Opposite above **NO. 61668 – DONCASTER STATION**

Approaching Doncaster station with a northbound freight during mid-1953 is no. 61668 *Bradford City*. Like classmate no. 61667 *Bradford*, no. 61668 had recently emerged from the works following a general repair and was being run in before returning to work at Stratford. Yet, in contrast to the engine's namesake, no. 61668 was equipped with a diagram 100A boiler and this occurred in June 1949 at Stratford. *Bradford City* had also acquired Westinghouse brake equipment in March 1941 at Gorton. Photograph by Geoff Warnes.

Opposite below **NO. 61668 – STRATFORD WORKS**

No. 61668 *Bradford City* had only very recently been withdrawn from service when pictured at Stratford Works on 23rd August 1960. The engine had been at Stratford shed for the final nine months in traffic, this being the last of several spells there from the late 1930s. Photograph by D.J. Dippie.

Above NO. 61670 – ARDLEIGH STATION

No. 61670 *City of London* was relieved of the streamlined casing during a general repair at Gorton over six months from October 1950 to April 1951; at the same time a diagram 100A boiler was fitted. The locomotive is at Ardleigh station on 9th October 1955 with an express. Yarmouth-allocated at this time, withdrawal from Lowestoft occurred in April 1960. Photograph courtesy Rail-Online.

Opposite above NO. 61669 – YARMOUTH SOUTH TOWN SHED

Taking on coal at Yarmouth South Town shed's coal stage in July 1955 is no. 61669 *Barnsley*. The engine is with 'The Easterling' headboard and this express ran from Liverpool Street to Lowestoft and Yarmouth, with only one stop at Beccles. No. 61669 was allocated to Ipswich for most of the BR period, lasting from April 1950 until condemned in September 1958. Photograph courtesy Rail-Online.

Opposite below NO. 61670 – NORWICH THORPE STATION

The first station in Norwich was opened by the Yarmouth & Norwich Railway in 1844. In the following year, the line from Brandon was completed and this later allowed a connection with Cambridge and London. By the end of the decade the station was renamed Norwich Thorpe, following the arrival of the Eastern Union Railway from Ipswich to Norwich Victoria station. At the start of the 1880s, increasing traffic saw plans formulated to rebuild Norwich Thorpe station. The project was completed by 1886 to the design of GER architect W.N. Ashbee and a cost of approx. £60,000. Modernisations were later carried out under BR, with a sixth platform added and new booking hall provided in the mid-1950s. No. 61670 *City of London* is at Norwich Thorpe station in the early 1950s with a local service. Photograph courtesy Rail-Online.

Below NO. 61671 – LIVERPOOL STREET STATION

Servicing of no. 61671 *Royal Sovereign* is carried out at Liverpool Street station in the early 1950s. The locomotive had received a fresh coat of LNER green in May 1950 following a general repair at Darlington; this also included the return of the painted cylinder sides. Interestingly, the Paint Shop there had not turned to BR green which had been applied to B17s from as early as 1949. A feature non-standard for other B2s and unique to no. 61671 is illustrated here. The engine appears to have been given a front smokebox ring from or influenced by the B16 Class as two footsteps are provided either side of the door at the bottom. The whole smokebox was a hybrid of features from the B1 Class and B17, with the original door retained (with GN-type top lamp iron), along with chimney.

Above NO. 61671 – MARSHMOOR

No. 61671 *Royal Sovereign* has a local train from Cambridge to King's Cross at Marshmoor on 11th July 1953. In BR green, the livery was likely first applied at Stratford after a general repair in early 1952. *Locomotives of the LNER Part 2B: Tender Engines – Classes B1 to B19* notes that no. 61671 was particularly troubled with frame problems from rebuilding, perhaps due to the retention of the original frames. From early 1946 to 1950, for example, the locomotive had ten out of course visits to Stratford Works, as well as two general repairs. Matters improved slightly during the 1950s, although the engine generally made two unscheduled visits to Stratford between general repairs. Another explanation for this could be the use as 'Royal' engine, meaning extra care was taken on the condition.

Above NO. 61672 – BRENTWOOD

When the first portion of the Eastern Counties Railway opened in 1840, the eastern temporary terminus for the line was at Brentwood. Financial difficulties slowed further work and not until 1843 was the route to Colchester open. The section from Liverpool Street to Shenfield – the next station eastward from Brentwood – was the subject of a suburban electrification scheme under the LNER, with the project completed in 1949. Running underneath the 1500V DC overhead lines at Brentwood in the mid-1950s is no. 61672 *West Ham United*. Photograph courtesy Rail-Online.

Below NO. 61672 – IPSWICH

Light engine in the Ipswich area during April 1954 is no. 61672 *West Ham United*. Allocated to Colchester at this time, a transfer to Stratford occurred in October 1955. At Ipswich from October 1958, the final move was to Lowestoft in June 1959 and withdrawal occurred there in March 1960. No. 61672 was fitted with Westinghouse brake equipment in April 1940 and had a diagram 100A boiler fitted in September 1950. Photograph courtesy Rail-Online.

BIBLIOGRAPHY

Allen, C.J. *Titled Trains of Great Britain.* 1983.

Dippie, D.J. *B17 & B2 Nameplates – 'Sandringhams' & Footballers.* Unpublished.

Gourvish, T.R. *British Railways 1948-73: A Business History.* 1986.

Griffiths, Roger and Paul Smith. *The Directory of British Engine Sheds and Principal Locomotive Servicing Points: 1 Southern England, the Midlands, East Anglia and Wales.* 1999.

Hawkins, Chris and George Reeve. *Great Eastern Railway Engine Sheds: Part Two Ipswich & Cambridge Districts.* 1987.

LNER Magazine – Various Issues.

Pike, S.N. *Mile by Mile on the LNER.* 1951.

Quick, Michael. *Railway Passenger Stations in Great Britain: A Chronology.* 2009.

RCTS. *Locomotives of the LNER Part 1: Preliminary Survey.* 1963.

RCTS. *Locomotives of the LNER Part 2B: Tender Engines – Classes B1 to B19.* 1975.

Swinger, Peter. *The Power of the B17s and B2s.* 1988.

Walmsley, Tony. *Shed by Shed Part Two: Eastern.* 2010.

Yeadon, W.B. *Yeadon's Register of LNER Locomotives Volume Five: Gresley B17 & Thompson B2 Classes.* 1993.

Also available from Great Northern

The Last Years of Yorkshire Steam	Western Steam 1948-1966
The Golden Age of Yorkshire Railways	The Last Years of North West Steam
Gresley's A3s	Gresley's V2s
Peppercorn's Pacifics	Southern Steam 1948-1967
London Midland Steam 1948-1966	Yorkshire Steam 1948-1967
The Last Years of North East Steam	Gresley's A4s
British Railways Standard Pacifics	John Ryan's Express

visit www.*greatnorthernbooks.co.uk* for details.